MACCLESFIELD DEMOLISHED

but not Forgotten

Memories of Macclesfield

by

Raymond Maddock

*Cover designed by
Brian Ollier*

CHURNET VALLEY BOOKS
1 King Street, Leek, Staffordshire. 01538 399033
email: picture.book@virgin.net web: freespace.virgin.net/c.hinton/
© Raymond Maddock and Churnet Valley Books 2000
ISBN 1 897949 70 7

Forward

Macclesfield of yesteryear. The stuff dreams are still made of. It is hard, perhaps even impossible, to define why there is such tremendous nostalgia for this wonderful and glorious town, yet there is. Just ask anyone born, bred or who has become a Maxonian and they will tell you that the town holds and hangs on to happy memories. It is an indisputable fact.

I have known Ray Maddock, the author of this book for many a year. I probably first came across him in the early 1960s when he was still very actively engaged in many organisations in the town and I was a cub reporter on the old Macclesfield Advertiser. Then, as I progressed to become editor of the Macclesfield Express, the name kept cropping up, but always in the same way; it was the name of a man who was doing something for the town he loved. Now I like to think of him as a good friend.

Ray Maddock has campaigned long and hard for Treacle Town, and has had more wins than losses against the faceless town planners who have done little or nothing for our town. He has taken on Red Tape, cut it and devoured it. He has been a champion of and for Maxonians. Now he is reliving and sharing his childhood and formative years and his many memories in this lavishly illustrated book. I have had the pleasure of seeing many of the photographs and have read much of his writing and can heartily recommend this work by a Son of Macclesfield for all Lovers of Macclesfield everywhere.

Doug Pickford,
Editor Macclesfield Express 1972-94

THIS BOOK IS DEDICATED TO THE PHOTOGRAPHIC SKILL OF THE LATE JACK RHODES

Acknowledgements

My thanks to John Crawford, David Hall, Susan Marsh, Brian Ollier, Doug Pickford, Jack Rhodes and Tony Sutton.

Contents

The author, 1956.

Preface

This book was written to record some of the recent history of Macclesfield - a pictorial record of buildings lost in the middle of the twentieth century with the purpose of trying to stimulate an interest in the young who would not remember the buildings lost, and nostalgia in those old enough to remember them.

It is hoped that the words and pictures will create a basis for discussion from the information presented by the author and even cause argument over the authenticity of some of the details. I also hope that it will serve as a reference book in years to come for those wishing to research the history of our town.

I wish to thank Tony Sutton for providing most of the pictures, taken by the late Jack Rhodes who up to his death resided at 3 Coare Street. The cover was designed by Brian Ollier, photographer, of the Palace Yard Studio in Mill Street, a long time friend.

I also give my thanks to Doug Pickford who encouraged me to write the book and to my niece, Susan Marsh, who transferred all the copy onto computer disc.

The memories and opinions expressed in this book are just my personal views put into print and should not be construed as facts. The dates and details have been taken from various sources and cannot necessarily be relied upon.

But I hope my thoughts will give you much pleasure. Read and enjoy it.

Raymond Maddock.

Hovis Factory Fires 1967. Viewed from Black Road.   Photograph Brian Ollier.

CHAPTER ONE
THE AUTHOR

I would ask you, when you read the book, to remember they are my memories; you may find that they differ from your own. It is well known that in old age we tend to forget some things and our minds often invent new slants on old experiences. I hope my observations will re-kindle old memories you have long since forgotten.

I was inspired to write this book when by good fortune a large number of old photographs came into my possession, many of which had never been seen by the public. I had often thought of writing a book about my life but decided that there was not enough in it for others to read, but I felt that these photographs, along with some of my own, would make interesting viewing, particularly for the older inhabitants of our lovely town.

I often look around and wonder if things would have been different had we had a different approach to the rebuilding and expansion of our old market town by the 'planners' after the ending of the Second World War. I watched as the town was destroyed piece by piece in the pursuit of progress and I came to the conclusion that much of the demolition was unnecessary. Many of our beloved buildings were needlessly destroyed. Two examples come to mind: Firstly the wholesale demolition of a community at the bottom of Hurdsfield Road to build the Victoria Park Flats. The flats are now being knocked down themsleves, even before, I believe, they have been paid for, to be replaced by 'more friendly' accommodation. It is a pity that the 'planners' did not take the advice at the time of the residents to renovate the properties. Rod Hackney did it on Black Road.

The second example was the demolition of the beautiful church on Statham Street, St. John's, to be replaced by a new monstrosity on Earlsway just because the population was on the move. The new church did not last long because of vandalism and the poor building materials used in its construction.

You may ask just what my qualifications are for writing a book on Macclesfield. My qualifications as a Maxonion are that I have lived in the town for in excess of sixty years. Although I admit to being born over a shop in Heaton Moor Stockport, I moved to the town at the age of three months. I spent my early childhood during the War years, not that I remember the War, in a four storey house at 157 Chester Road. This was a large red brick building, part of 155 Chester Road which was occupied by a Mr Dakin and his family, a local decorator. This house has been demolished only to be replaced by an inferior red brick block of flats. Whilst my home overlooked farmland belonging to Mr Brocklehurst (who had a son John and two daughters Thelma and Dorothy), the present building overlooks the fire and ambulance station and the new Territorial Army Headquarters.

At an early age my parents did not get along too well, and after they split up we were evicted for non-payment of rent. Along with my brother and sister and two step sisters we finished up in a one roomed house in Shaw Street. Fortunately after only a few nights we were able to move to an upstairs flat above 12 Beech Lane.

Up to this point I have very few memories of the town but I started to notice things around me soon after when we moved to a shop at 20 Cross Street, rented from Mr Pickford who ran the shop at 22 selling greengrocery. My mother kept myself and my younger brother and sister by selling secondhand clothes and furniture in the shop. I was being educated at Athey Street School and walked to and from the school every day although only nine at the time. I was able enough to pass the eleven plus and soon after moving to a house at 193 Park Lane my move to the Kings School was made.

I remained at Park Lane until 1968. After spending many happy childhood days and my early working days there I moved to 120 Windmill Street. There, in addition to the large house known as Shawleigh, I built a bungalow in the grounds and with my interest in alternative lifestyles I designed and built the Country's first autonomous house. At that time I was also advising the local branch of Friends of the Earth on such things as global warming, of course now very popular. I later abandoned the project - it was ahead of its time - and moved to land at Lyme Green where I have stayed and where some time in the future I expect to be buried.

The author in the RAF

During my life I have served in the RAF as a fireman, doing National Service; I have been the Scoutmaster at the 9th Macclesfield St. John's troop for many years; I have been President of the Macclesfield and District Riding Club, and on the committees of the East Cheshire Combined Training Group and Chairman of the Riding for the Disabled Committee. I was Treasurer of the Parkside Social Club, and of the Civil Defence Social Club until it was disbanded.

In 1963 I spent three months in America as a camp councillor at the invitation of the American Government, travelling from Washington to Niagara along the eastern seaboard. In the 1970's I travelled extensively on the Continent as a coach driver getting as far as Turkey amongst the fifty five countries that I visited.

Despite all this travel I always felt that Macclesfield was home, the place to which I would always return. During my lifetime, prior to my retirement to concentrate on my interest in conservation, I worked as a screen printer's assistant at Lower Heyes Mill, an office clerk at Firesnow Ltd on Withyfold Drive, an aircraft fire-fighter at Gaydon on the A34 between Warwick and Banbury (now a national motor museum); a wages clerk in the Health Service mostly at Parkside Hospital; a lorry driver for Carswells Parcels on Black Lane; a salesman for Conlowes in Congleton; a driving school operator; and, for the last twenty eight years, a coach operator and part time farmer.

I feel my experiences give me some insight into the recent history of our beloved town. In the chapters that follow I will express my concern over the disappearance of some of what I believe was our architectural heritage.

CHAPTER TWO
CHURCHES AND CHAPELS

I will start with places of worship in the town. Some preceded the factories but many followed the expansion of the local economy as the area changed from a rural centre, based on its market, to an industrial centre, particularly of the silk industry.

The largest group of churches is referred to as the Church of England following Henry VIII's altercation with the Pope, and are named after saints. Most have schools attached to them, many of which survived well into the second half of the twentieth century when they were largely replaced as larger places of education were built to facilitate the secondary education of an increasing population. Loss of the smaller church schools accelerated as successive governments went for comprehensive education, the abolition of the eleven plus exam, and the adoption of a bigger is better attitude.

The church of St. Michael's by the Town Hall is the most prominent and well known but does not appear to have had a school. There has been a place of worship on this site for a great many years; I believe the original chapel was the sixth oldest in the country. St Michael's church was founded in 1278 by Queen Eleanor seventeen years after her husband had granted this obscure hamlet of Macclesfield corporate status by charter.

St. Paul's church in Brook Street, St. Peters in Windmill Street, St. Andrews on the corner of St. Andrews Road and Brough Street West and St. George's in St. George's Place between High Street and St. George's Street, all had schools alongside them. Holy Trinity Church on Hurdsfield Road also had its own school next door, a place I well remember for its Scottish country dancing when I was a teenager.

Christ Church is an odd one, now defunct and having half of the its gravestones removed to make way for 'another' car park. This church was built, according to the history books, of red brick in only nine months on a hill outside the town. It was built by Charles Roe on behalf of a curate of St. Michael's, the Reverend David Simpson, who had split with his church as his method of preaching was not appreciated. The church was originally known as the 'new church'. It opened on Christmas day 1775 and soon proved very popular with the public. The Reverend Simpson was responsible for starting education for the less well off, the beginning of education for all in Macclesfield.

All these churches, with the exception of Christ Church, still survive today, but I suspect with much reduced congregations. They have all lost their schools over the years, many of the buildings being turned into living accommodation.

The Catholics seem to have only two churches in Macclesfield, one on Chester Road, St. Albans, which did have its own school across the road, and St. Edward's on London Road, which as far as I know, did not have a school although there is a new school nearby which takes the same name - I do not think that its intake is restricted to Catholics. Both these churches seem thriving places of worship today. The Roman Catholics in the town first worshipped in rooms, the former residence of the Duke of Buckingham, in 1792. A school was built in 1810 on Chester Road and used as a church until St. Albans was opened in 1841. St. Edward's came later.

The Methodists have seen many of their churches closing down during my lifetime, and are now centralised under the roof of one new church built in Westminster Road. One of the first to go was Trinity Church in Cumberland Street; I remember it particularly well as I was involved in its demise as assistant to Blaster Bates who was employed to oversee the downfall of its beautiful spire. The site is now occupied by sheltered housing.

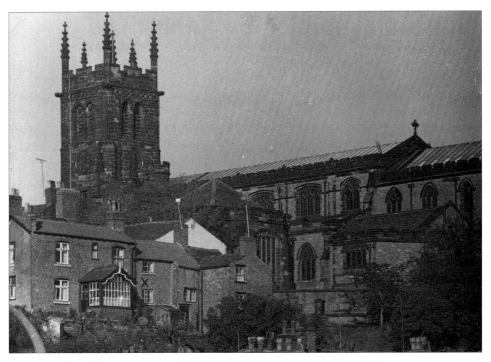

A view of St Michael's church from Waters Green with the top of the 108 steps just visible.

St. Michael's church built 1278. The picture would have been taken about 1960. Note milk lorry in the background with churns aboard.

St. Andrew's church.

Christ Church after exhumation of most of the graves to create car parking.

Another important loss was the Wesleyan Chapel in Sunderland Street opposite the bus station. This was built in 1780, the first of many chapels to be built in the town, although the Methodists did have a meeting house in Commercial Road as early as 1764.

Two of the Methodists' largest chapels, both with extensive church rooms attached, were Brunswick in Chapel Street, and Newtown in South Park Road. In my earlier days I attended both. First I went to the Newtown Sunday School in Hatton Street but later left them as they did not have a scout troop and joined Brunswick who did. Here I attained the rank of patrol leader of the Peewits under the watchful eyes of Billy Richardson the Group Scoutmaster and Phil Tittensor the Scoutmaster. I recall the other patrol leader was Les Crohn who later ran a flower shop in Mill Lane. I enjoyed my scouting days at Brunswick and well recall attending camp at Bangor along with the St. James troop lead by George Foot and assisted by Mr and Mrs Shaw, two very well known Sutton residents.

There was a Methodist Chapel on Stamford Road, Moss Estate, and one on Beech Lane, a new building following the re-routing of the inner ring road. As I have said, many of these chapels have been incorporated into the one new chapel built in 1999 in Westminster Road on the old site of Young's builders' yard.

We lost Fence Methodists when the area was cleared to make way for the notorious Victoria Park flats. The Ebenezer Chapel in Higher Hurdsfield still exists as a place of worship. There was a small chapel in Tabor Street between Saville Street and Copper Street although in the later years it was used as a retail outlet for camping gear.

In 1951 St. John's Sunday School building, formerly St. John's school, built in 1869, at the junction of South Park Road and Hatton Street, was used as the headquarters of a new scout group, the 9th Macclesfield under the leadership of Mr Whittaker and Mr Rose. As this was much nearer my home I left the Brunswick troop and joined the St. John's. As neither of the leaders had been scouts prior to the setting up of the group I found myself acting as Scoutmaster at the age of fifteen. I later went on to Gilwell and on reaching the age of eighteen I was officially made the Scout leader.

During my time at St. John's there were many changes. The old Vicar Reverend Robinson, Robo as he was known to us, retired and was replaced by The Reverend W. Lakeland, straight from church training. He proved very unpopular, changing the church service and alienating the whole of the church choir. I recall their resignation under the leadership of Mr Yearsley, choirmaster and organist, whose son Keith went on to make quite a name for himself as a choirmaster and headmaster.

Around this time I was the youngest member of the Parochial Church Council when a decision was taken to close down the lovely old church in Statham Street and build a new one on Earlsway. I still recall the meeting where we were told that the repairs to the old church would cost £7000 and the cost of building a new church £21,000. A model of the proposed new church was produced and the architect came to the meeting. The Parochial Church Council were persuaded that the future lay on the Weston Estate. The vote was not unanimous as I voted against the move, as not in the best interest of the scout group. It meant boundary changes which would put the Scout headquarters outside the parish and would cause problems on church parades because of the distance for a marching band.

The foundation stone of the new church was laid in August 1961 but during construction the interior was spoilt by a late addition of a steel cable right across the centre to stop the walls from bulging. This cut across the eyeline of the whole congregation when looking up at the newly carved statue of Jesus Christ!

When the church did move, the diocesan authorities no longer had a use for the old school, and the parents committee of the scout troop raised the money to buy it. Once it

Newtown Chapel built 1873. The building to the right is Mafeking Hall originally St. John's school.

Mount Tabor Chapel. At the time of the picture it was used as a camp shop. Note the post office van when the telephone system was still part of the post office.

Mafeking Hall. Formerly St. John's school built 1869.

Salvation Army Citadel, Roe Street.

became the property of the group I christened the building Mafeking Hall, the name it still carries today. The name was inspired by the actions of Baden Powell in South Africa during the Boer War as described in his book *Scouting for Boys*.

There are of course places of worship for other denominations. The Salvation Army had their citadel in Mill Street next to the Majestic Cinema in a building originally a theatre. It was later demolished to make way for a shopping arcade and the Salvation Army moved to a building in Roe Street, formerly a place of worship for various religions.

There is a Unitarian Chapel on King Edward Street, built as a meeting place for dissenters from the Church of England in 1690. I do not know its full history but it probably would make very interesting reading. It can still be seen today, and it holds services; its access is up a narrow entry between the old police station and Blunt's solicitors.

The building in Roe Street currently occupied by the Salvation Army has a very interesting history. It was built in 1829 apparently due to a break with Christ Church. Just as Christ Church broke away from St. Michael's, it seems that a member of the clergy at Christ Church was dismissed for a liaison with a female parishioner. He set up the new church along with a large part of Christ Church's congregation who supported him. When this church joined the Congregational Church on Park Green to become the United Reform Church the building in Roe Street was sold off to St. Albans Catholic Church who put in a dance floor and used it as a social centre. Many of you may have attended dances there.

During the War the building was occupied by the Americans and after they left it was left empty for some time, eventually being put to good use by the Salvation Army who vacated their premises in Mill Street. There may have been a financial attraction as their old Citadel was later to be demolished for another shopping precinct. The new Citadel has been used as the setting for a T.V. series about religion, the interior shots being made at the church in St. George's Street. I think the T.V. series was called *Mr Roe's Virgins*.

There is also the St. Barnabas Mission on Lime Avenue, where as a youth I attended many social functions. This building was I believe attached to St. George's Church. There was a Mission in Mill Street at the junction of Pickford Street commonly referred to as the Town Mission. I never knew much about the building as it stood back from the road, isolated beyond forbidding iron gates. I always thought that it was where homeless people went for shelter but this could well have been just my imagination. The last time I looked it was a night club called 'Preachers'!

Bethel Baptist church still survives on Heapy Street, or Calamine Square as it was known, long after all the small cottages that were there have been replaced by industrial buildings, leaving the church somewhat isolated.

The other Baptist chapel I recall was at the Park Street end of St. George's Street, used as I said in recent years as a set for a television series. This building proudly displays the date it was built, MDCCCXXIII - 1823 I think - only one year after the Lord Street Sunday School, now the home of the Macclesfield Amateur Dramatic Society's Little Theatre.

Hurdsfield had its very own Carisbrook Chapel, home of the Christian Brethren, and Parkside had its own church, St. Lukes, administered from Henbury Parish Church, now sadly taken over by Macclesfield's largest builder of houses and likely to become flats since its demolition has been opposed. It has been very badly vandalised and may yet have to be demolished due to neglect.

St. Michael's had its parish rooms opposite the Kings School main gates, affectionately known as the tin tabernacle although not used as far as I know by the Jewish faith - they met over a shop in Chestergate.

Bethel Baptist Church,
Heapy Street.

Baptist Chapel,
St George's Street,
built 1872.

In Church Street West, tucked away behind a new filling station on Churchill Way, there is an old church building dating back to 1842. It is now used as offices and part of it has been demolished to make room for the staff to park their cars.

Harvest Printers on Park Lane between High Street and James Street was, I recall, a house of worship until it fell into disuse and was taken over by a printing firm who lost no time in having the adjoining graveyard exhumed to make way for a car park.

There was a place of worship on Byron Street, a lovely red brick building, demolished along with all the surrounding houses, and a very good chip shop, to make way for new properties. I do not know why they had to go when similar properties to the north of Byron Street were saved - they were renovated and classed as a conservation area. It seems a pity they could not all have been saved. I did benefit from the demolition of those between Byron Street and White Street. The contractors, Hobson and Sons, sold me some of the very heavy timbers used as roof supports. I still know the whereabouts of some of those timbers which I originally incorporated into the house I built on Windmill Street.

A lesser known church is that of the Spiritualists Free Church in Cumberland Street. This building whose foundation stone was laid in 1879 is tucked away between two houses and behind a row of conifers which, with Cumberland Street being cut in half by the new road and hence now a cul de sac, makes it almost invisible. It still holds regular services.

Churches have been built in my lifetime. One, erected about 1945, was the Elim Pentecostal Church between Pool Street and Old Mill Lane. I do not know the history of the sect but I think prior to the opening they met in a house around the Lowe Street area.

There is a new church at the junction of Victoria Road and Priory Lane called The Church of Jesus Christ and Latterday Saints (or Mormons) and one at the Ivy Road end of Earlsway called Calvary Church - and I must not forget the one on Earlsway built to the glory of St. John the Evangelist to replace the one only built in 1961 and later demolished.

There has not been a synagogue in the town now for a number of years but there was once one at 62 Chestergate. During the last War a number of Jewish workers in the clothing trade left the East End of London for a safer place in Macclesfield. One of their number was Joshua Cohen who purchased Holland and Barwoods shop in Chestergate, where the family sold soft furnishing for many years. Joshua set up the synagogue in Chestergate and between 1941 and 1946 the Jewish faith was practised there. After the end of the War many of the refugees returned to London and the church was abandoned. The Cohen family however stayed on in the town and Joshua's two sons attended the Kings School at the same time as I did and both made their names in the town, one serving as a magistrate.

Finally there is a church which seems to be still thriving, the United Reform Church on Park Green. It has a building to the rear in Townley Street which is regularly used by various youth organisations. My memory of this building was learning to play badminton under the instruction of the caretaker's daughter. The Townley Street building was erected in 1788 as a sunday school and is still home to brownies and scouts amongst others.

There is a small church building in the grounds of the cemetery which was recently taken over and is now used as an office, but at least it did survive the bulldozer. There is also the well-known building of the 'Large Sunday School' built with the money of Charles Roe and now called the Heritage Centre. This was opened in 1796 as a sunday school. The records tell us that between March 1814 and June 1815 nearly $2^{1/2}$ thousand children were educated within its walls.

I expect there will be churches I have missed due to my memory - which also does not recall a mosque, but I am sure that is only a matter of time.

St Luke's, Parkside, boarded up, with holes in the roof and stained glass windows broken.

Church Street West, built 1842.

Spiritualist Free Church, Cumberland Street.

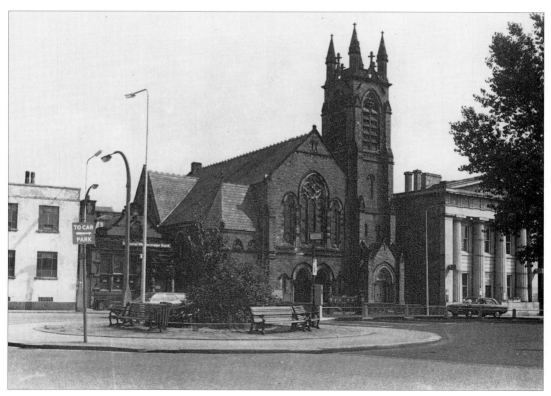

Congregational Church, Park Green, 1877, now called the United Reform Church.

Townley Street Sunday School.

Large Sunday School, Roe Street. Cost to build, £5,639.13s.1d.

CHAPTER THREE
FACTORIES OF THE TOWN

Macclesfield has a long history; an early staging post for the Roman Legions as they marched from Buxton to Chester; a Charter Borough since 1261; visited by Bonnie Prince Charlie; an important place for the distribution of salt from the areas of Nantwich, Middlewich and Northwich; and a market town which continued to prosper during the period of the industrial revolution when some very clever men like Charles Roe made Macclesfield the centre of the world silk industry.

Many factories grew up around the town in this period of boom and alongside them the many rows of cottages for the workers. A few of these cottages remain, some with the third storey garrets where home workers produced the finest of threads. The factories predominantly produced silk, but many associated trades developed such as ribbon and button making. There were also the foundries and engineering shops that went with the silk industry. All the factories operated for long hours and the bosses certainly exploited the workers. In many places whole families, including young children, worked long hours to survive, had little or no education and their life expectancy was poor.

During the period from 1960 onwards the factories in the town faced strong opposition from cheap imports and many were forced to adapt or close. With the growth in plastics and the new electronic age a few have adapted but many went to the wall as the competition became too great.

In the 1970s it seemed to me that a large number of factories were being demolished, but just as many seemed to be destroyed by fire. The numbers involved seemed to be so great that I cannot help but feel that a professional arsonist was making a good living in the town. Empty factories, and some still just scraping a living, seemed to be going up in smoke at an alarming rate. Maybe fire was cheaper and quicker than demolition and certainly more profitable if the insurance could be claimed!

The number of buildings lost is considerable but I will try to recall some of those I remember; those demolished, those burnt down by accident or design and also some of those which still survive today.

Probably the first factory to produce silk in the town would have been one on Park Green next to the Congregational Church. This was demolished to make way for new buildings. At one stage it was a retail outlet for frozen food products but now the site is predominantly covered by Silk House containing the County Court offices. This moved from the office block which had replaced the old brewery on Park Green, demolished once the brewing of beer had ceased.

I remember Brocklehurst Whiston Amalgamated situated on Hurdsfield Road extending around the corner onto Fence Avenue. I recall the entrance through a very small and uninviting doorway where on occasions I met my sister after work - she had a clerical job there. B.W.A. as it was generally known had a disastrous fire in 1975 which destroyed a large part of the factory on the Fence Avenue side.

The rest of the factory was demolished to make way for Simister's Ford garage to move their operation from on Hibel Road with ATS alongside them. I recall well the demolition as I was the owner of the site where all the rubble from the factory foundations was tipped.

Of the large number of silk mills in the town one of the best known was that of Heath's in Pickford Street. I am sure many of you will remember the bridge across the street

The demolition of Macclesfield's first silk mill in the early seventies.

Brocklehurst Whiston's office entrance, Hurdsfield Road.

connecting the two parts of the factory. I remember the factory because during the short period I drove for Carswell Parcels, then in Black Lane and later in North Rode, I used to do deliveries there. This factory fell victim to the heavy ball and chain of the demolition men in 1976. Although the factory went, many of the buildings around it survived. Many of them fell later to make way for the car park at Normid, itself, so we hear, soon to be demolished to make way for a cinema and bus station. Sunderland Street itself is in a sorry state of neglect following the closure of Gas Road and the opening of the Silk Road. It seems only a matter of time, as council policy blights the area, to its demise.

Probably the most easily recognised factory in the town is Frost Mill on Park Green. The factory was taken over by a new industry to the town under the name of Gradus, who I think started out by making aluminium stair edgings and have over the years built up a worldwide reputation. To their credit they have kept the factory, which overlooks the Cenotaph on Park Green, in its original state along with the old clock, still in working order and maintained by an old friend of mine, Keith Hamilton, plumber and chief maintenance man. The part of the factory which extended around the corner onto Mill Lane was damaged by a fire which brought traffic to a standstill as onlookers watched it burn whilst the fire brigade made a valiant effort to save it. The damage was so extensive that the upper stories were lost and factory was rebuilt as a two storey building.

One of the towns most spectacular fires was that at the Hovis Mill on Union Road. I was at the time travelling up Brook Street and saw the flames leaping from the roof before the fire brigade arrived. I immediately contacted my friend Brian Ollier who came and took photographs and had the film on the train at Central Station in time for the Manchester Evening News' evening edition. The Hovis factory was the main administration centre for Hovis bread and did not produce, as far as I am aware, any bread despite the entrance for flour barges from the canal. A local hero, Rod Hackney architect and friend of Prince Charles, has more recently turned the factory into living space.

Many of our old factories have survived both fire and demolition and they are some of our best examples of architecture. I expect some of them will now stay with us, given a use can be found for them, and outlive places like Stuart House in King Street, the new town hall extension and our multi storey car parks, all of whose architecture leaves much to be desired.

One fine example is the Regency Mill, more commonly known as the Card Factory. The Mill was built 1775 and its magnificent clock allowed locals to check the time of day for years before the digital wrist watch became popular. In 1982 the cottages opposite the front of the mill were demolished to make way for a new road to alleviate traffic at the junction between Chester Road and Chestergate.

The Royal Silk Warehouse just off Waters Green stands proudly looking out over the railway line towards the Derbyshire Hills and Buxton. I shall always remember the building as the Castle Shoe Company although in more recent times occupied by A.W. Clowes. Over the years many large cranes have been seen lifting machinery into and out of the building, too large to negotiate the stairs or lifts.

One of the smallest factories to go was the one at the junction of Baker Street and Bread Street, that's between Crompton Road and Peter Street. With an address like that you might think that it was a bakery; well maybe it was once but at the time I discovered it, it was a bubble pipe factory. It had ceased production and was derelict. As a boy of thirteen I was attracted to the empty building, so I climbed the rear gate and entered the unsecured building and was amazed to find tray after tray of china clay pipes in various stages of

Brocklehurst Whiston's, burnt
down in 1975.

Brocklehurst Whiston's, Fence
Avenue, after the fire.

Heath's Silk Mill Pickford Street 1970.

Demolition of Heath's Silk Mill, Pickford Street, 1976.

production. Everything was covered in dust so it had been deserted some time before. It was like entering the Marie Celeste, abandoned in mid production.

Most of the pipes were broken but a search through the rubble revealed many unbroken pipes some with long stems and known as churchwarden pipes. I used the booty to learn for the first time the art of smoking. Since it was illegal to buy tobacco I had to do with the "dog ends" I could find - in anycase I could not afford cigarettes not even a pack of Little Willys Wild Woodbines!

I will not reveal my accomplices on the forays into the old mill, but they know who they were. If you did not live in the area you would not know of its existence and now it has gone so it is too late to discover the secrets of Macclesfield's pipe factory.

On London Road we still have two factories, which have survived as small industrial units. I suspect that their survival owes something to their position alongside the River Bollin. One known as Byrom House is occupied, amongst others, by East Cheshire Glass and Aquarius Health and Fitness Studios. When these factories were built we were not a car owning society, so no provision was made for parking. The Council in their wisdom have created a car park alongside them for those wishing to walk along the River Bollin pathway, but I am not aware that you can actually walk from this car park along the Bollin in either direction - anyway it is always full of vehicles in connection with Byrom House.

The other factory known as Albion Mill stands near to the public house of the same name - I think an old name for England. This too is split into smaller units one of which is Legend Products. When I was a young man I recall this firm, which has since become a worldwide name, starting the manufacture of plaster models. A very nice young lady with whom I was acquainted, worked in the office there. We were later to appear in local pantomime together and she went on to own a very successful dancing school.

As I was compiling my list of factories it did seem that a large number were on the edge of the River Bollin, which incidentally does not run through Bollington, at least not the one close to Macclesfield. It may have been that the atmosphere close to the water was suitable for the making of silk in the same way as the Lancashire hills suited the manufacture of cotton. It might have just been the availability of space as houses were built away from the river for safety perhaps. Whatever the reason it was not, as far as I am aware, the need to drive the factories with water power, although perhaps the mills were built on the sites of former mills which did use the river as an energy source.

There is a factory between Waterside and Windmill Street known a Victoria Mill which is currently occupied by Gardiner Caldwell Communications although I will always remember it as Windsmoors. They made ladies skirts, when I lived in Park Lane. My mother was a home worker for Windsmoor and had regular deliveries of skirts. I spent many hours picking off the loose ends of cotton whilst my mother sewed in the labels on the waistbands prior to collection the following day.

A factory which was built and then demolished in my lifetime was the Umbro factory on Hulley Road. It was built where the old Bollington Railway line was crossed by a farm road over a narrow bridge to the Red Barn. Many will not remember the Red Barn but most will recall the bridge, which provided access to the estate from Tytherington for many years, with its set of traffic lights. It was later replaced by the roundabout on the Silk Road.

Umbros was a very modern factory built around a smaller factory of which the name escapes me, but which made specialist equipment for the engineering industry. This small firm came to the town from Watford along with most of its own staff. One family, Mr and Mrs Baldry, lived at 6 Gawsworth Road with their son and daughter and became good

Frost Mill, Park Green 1976.

Frost Mill, Park Green, before their fire.

Frost Mill, Mill Lane, after the fire which later made it two storey.

Card Factory, Regency Mill, built 1775. Pictured 1982 when the site around was cleared to make way for a road between Oxford Road and Cumberland Street connecting the Talbot Hotel to the Park Hotel

Royal Silk Warehouse, known as Castle Shoe Co.

Byrom House, London Road.

friends of mine but on retirement they moved back south to be with their family.

Umbros had their head office in Wilmslow and the number of workers was so great that the firm provided buses to pick up the staff. I was often called upon to assist McCarthy Coaches as a part-time driver to ferry the workers to the Moss Estate via the bus station. I seem to remember they also at one point traded as Bukta and made camping clothing. This modern factory, occupied by a firm still very much in business if not in Macclesfield, was demolished to make way for another electrical retail outlet. Even as I write, yet another modern factory on Queens Avenue, Hurdsfield Estate, has just been demolished only to be rebuilt on the same site. It says very little for the standards of building. They engineer parts and equipment for the motor industry.

One factory which survived demolition during the building of the Victoria Park Flats was that of W.K. Lowe in Queen Street but it did later succumb to a car park when the firm found more suitable premises in Albert Road Bollington. I had on occasions driven the coach to get workers to Bollington from the old site on Commercial Road. I think that the new factory has already been abandoned and may well now be a site for new houses.

Bridge Street Mill stands on the corner of Bridge Street and Union Street and if my memory is correct was severely damaged by fire whilst operating as Peter Davenport's mill.

In Buckley Street, AWH Ltd (Hewetsons) had a factory which was built in 1932 and extended right through into Vincent Street. I remember Buckley Street well, then cobbled and with no parked cars, as it was there that I first rode a motor bike. It was a Francis Barnett owned by Barry Truman who lived in the street. Hewetsons have long gone but the building still exists and amongst other things it has been used for the production of stair edgings. It now looks very much ready for demolition as it is in a run-down state.

Lower down Vincent Street just past the rear of the B & Q building, which replaced the old Premier Cinema and Hydes Garage with its two lonely petrol pumps at the road side, is C and S Vincent Mill 1926. It is used by Mike Twigg as a very successful joiners shop. Do you know what C and S stood for? I cannot remember.

On the other side of Vincent Street and a little lower down was another large factory which went right through to Rodney Street. This building stood empty for years awaiting demolition. Now the factory is being put through a machine and ground up for recycling following a fire. This was the dyehouse of Thomas Crewe.

Another factory I passed on my way to school at Athey Street, when I lived in Cross Street, was that at the top of Hobson Street facing onto the park. It always had the clatter of machinery when I passed it. I do not suppose that children of today at the age of nine would be allowed to walk so far to school on their own! The mill I refer to was naturally called Park Mill and was built in 1852. I think it became a boat builder's yard for a time but has more recently been renovated.

Oberland Silk Mill on Mill Road still survives despite its regular changes of use. It was at one point Adamley Textiles but now at least part of it is called Venture House and is split into smaller units. The mill extends around Cross Street into Half Street but is, like so many, plagued with the dreaded parked car. Internally the factory has undergone much change but the frontage, apart from the Cross Street side which I could see from my bedroom when I lived at number 20, seems to have changed little.

A good example of a surviving mill is that in Old Park Lane, or now Park Lane as the council insist on calling it. This beautiful building may have been one of Smales, but is remembered by me as that of Halle Models Ltd, Lingerie. It is currently occupied by Arighi Bianchi as storage and warehousing. On the other side of Old Park Lane is a factory still

Albion Mill, London Road.

Oberland Silk Mill, Mill Road Sutton, still in use. Part of it is now Venture House.

in production as a museum and if you have not yet visited it you should.

Some factories did not survive. Neckwear in Grosvenor Street - I do not know exactly what they made but the name suggests it was silk ties - went under the hammer to make way for yet another council car park as the car was about to become king.

The large factory in St. George's Street, I think perhaps another of Smales, fell in 1974 to make way for 'affordable housing', which may not survive as long as the old factory did.

Further south in Pitt Street was another building referred to as the 'Old Ribbon Mills' and now converted to flats in the High Street conservation area.

I remember three other factories destroyed by the dreaded flames. A large factory used as a paper mill in Heapy Street was destroyed by fire. The land became a haulage yard. Union Mill in Statham Street was to be demolished along with all the surrounding cottages. The area was known as The Dams, where all the houses had high stone Macclesfield steps to keep out the water when the Dams Brook overflowed. But Union Mill Burnt down before it could be demolished. Maybe it was cheaper to burn it down, or better for insurance purposes, or just an unlucky coincidence due to tramps or careless teenagers with matches. Either way it went, as many others had done, on 28th October, leaving another pile of ash.

The third fire , which sticks in my memory most vividly, was Brodies Mill on Duke Street just to the rear of the Majestic Cinema, now a council car park. I was on my way to school on a quiet Monday morning when the site of the smoke made me divert from my normal route. Needless to say I did not reach the Kings School that day. It was very exciting to watch the firemen struggle to control the blaze. Little did I know then that one day I would be a fireman! I visited the site frequently after the fire and like many other boys was seen sporting little metal studs in my lapel and on my cap, booty retrieved from the ashes. The rumour was at the time that the owner of the mill was seen boarding the midnight express train to London on the night of the fire and that it had started at more than one point in the factory. Macclesfield has many stories about factory owners turning to arson due to the dwindling returns on their investments. Many would have considered this way of avoiding bankruptcy so I suspect at least some of the rumours would have been based on the truth.

In Bond Street, extending all the way round into Henderson Street and Newton Street, stands Kershaw Mill, named I presume after a Mr Kershaw. Unlike some of the towns factories Kershaws was built of a beautiful red brick of superior quality which may explain why it has avoided demolition. I remember the mill as that of F. Harding Ltd and on closer inspection I find it is still Harding Specialist Yarn Processors having been run now by three generations of the Harding family.

J. Dunckerley's Mill Stands on Oxford Road and extends around the corner into Cottage Street. Its height has been reduced with the removal of the top storey in the Cottage Street part but it still remains in use by a number of firms, most notably Monks, makers of pine furniture. Its survival is remarkable since its near neighbour on the opposite side of Oxford Road at the junction with Francis Street was totally demolished to make way for houses and to improve visibility around the bend in Oxford Road for the motorist, in which it did not really succeed.

A factory of Josiah Smale stood in George Street alongside the River Bollin and was demolished in 1975. This very large mill ran the length of George Street and into Brook Street straddling the River Bollin at one point. The mill cut out the daylight to the river carrying the clear waters from Shuttlinsloe and the surrounding hills with their sticklebacks and kingfishers. Here between the mills and the railway line it provided a convenient dumping ground for old bicycle frames and supermarket trolleys.

A notable fire damaged a factory in Thorpe Street along the River Bollin, one of two factories in the street. It went up in a cloud of smoke when it was occupied I think by Berrisford's (of Congleton) ribbon factory. It may also have been used at one point by Frank Stonely and Sons. It perished in April 1960 and was later rebuilt as four office units known now as Thorpe House. The second factory still stands and is partly used by the local council in connection with their street cleaning operations.

Strange as it seems Mill Street in Macclesfield never had a mill in it in my time although what was reputed to be the first silk mill in the town did stand at the foot of Mill Street. There are of course many other mills I have not mentioned; I expect some of them will have memories for you.

Last remaining tall chimney, that of Thomas Crewe, dismantled February 2000.

Smale's Silk Mill, Old Park Lane, one time Halle Models.

St. George's Street Mill, start of demolition to make way for houses.

Neckwear Grosvenor Street. Demolished early 1970's to make way for a car park.

Neckwear, Grosvenor Street.

Heapy Street Paper mill during the fire.

Union Mill, Statham Street destroyed by fire 28th October 1982.

Kershaw Mill, Newton Street.

Smale's Mill, Brook Street.
Start of demolition 1975.

Smale's Mill, George Street 1974.

CHAPTER FOUR
SCHOOLS AND HOSPITALS

Macclesfield has undergone many changes over the past forty years, not all of them for the better. We have seen the outdoor market moved around so that it no longer has a settled home; if something is not done soon it may be lost forever. We have seen the Town, and in particular Chestergate, cut in half by the inner relief road, Churchill Way as it has been named. We have had the Grosvenor shopping centre replace many of our traditional shops. We have had the pedestrianisation of first Chestergate and then Mill Street, and although maybe it was desirable, it has only served to make Macclesfield look like any other town in the Country. We have seen a move to large supermarkets on the fringe of the town and what was a planned industrial estate turned into a retail park. The domination of valuable land by one company has pushed land prices beyond the resources of many small businesses.

Our schools and hospitals have made the change from 'small is wasteful' to 'big is beautiful'. When I went to Athey Street junior school we occupied the lower storey of the building and one half of the playground. We put up with outside toilets and we all knew just where our futures lay. Athey Street juniors along with a large number of smaller schools, many attached to churches, took children from the age of about five to the age of eleven. At this point we were all subjected to the dreaded eleven plus examination. Those who passed went to the Kings School if they were boys; the girls went to the High School of Fence Avenue. The rest went to the secondary modern schools. In the case of Athey Street they just went upstairs to what was then called Park Royal along with children from many of the smaller schools. Those who lived on the other side of the town went to the Central School, boys and girls separated into upstairs and downstairs, with a divided playground at break times. This old school is now a junior school under the name of St. Barnabas.

There were a few exceptions to this rule but by and large all the over elevens were spread between the four big schools.

Over the years things started to change largely due to the expanding population. Most of the church schools closed down and were replaced by modern prefab-type buildings often keeping the same name. The Kings School and the High School became more elitist and took pupils from the surrounding towns. Macclesfield started to build new secondary modern schools. Up sprang Ryles Park, built on the farmland of Joe Torr, then Henbury and Tytherington, and latterly Fallibroome, and specially for those of the Catholic faith, All Hallows.

I do not know if it was that the education authority could not add up but at one stage Macclesfield was so short of senior school places it was bussing pupils to Poynton and Holmes Chapel. Things do seem to have improved now and recently there was a proposal to close Ryles Park school due to falling numbers. The High School was closed down - I am at a loss to know why as it was an excellent school. I suspect it may have been a political move but nevertheless this beautiful building stood empty for years with no one knowing what to do with it. Demolition seemed an option. The success of the Kings School was such that they introduced an intake for girls and later they were to re open the old girls' High School to cope with the numbers wanting a grammar school education.

Unlike the beautiful buildings of the old High School and the Kings School, all the new schools, Ryles Park, Henbury and Tytherington, were of similar design and are not likely to last too long. Fallibroome was built by Seddons to a much higher standard. Whilst

Trinity Church School Hurdsfield, demolished 1976.

I suspect Fallibroome, close to the boundary of Prestbury, along with the leisure centre and the new running track, were all needed, I wonder who was the idiot who decided on the location with its one very poor access from the road network.

For a short period prior to the opening of All Hallows school, in October 1962, girls who passed the eleven plus and were Catholic were permitted to opt for a place at the Convent school of Mount Carmel in Alderley Edge.

We still have a large number of junior schools which now seem to be referred to as county junior and county primary schools. The ones I can remember are Bollinbrook, Puss Bank, Ivy Bank, St. Edward's, Athey Street, St. Barnabas, Ash Grove, Marlborough, Hurdsfield, St. John's, St. Albans, Broken Cross and Upton Priory. At least one of these, the one on Brocklehurst Way, Hurdsfield, was built on poor ground and had to be demolished after a few years to be replaced at the same location. I do hope the new one lasts a little longer. It is clear to me that due to the design and standard of construction, and I presume financial restraint, most of these buildings will need to be replaced long before the need to demolish structures such as the High School and Kings.

Those who had occasion to travel up Chester Road would have seen and heard the children in the playground next to the old building of Broken Cross School. The school was demolished and the site was for many years in the hands of Burgess's agricultural engineers, but is currently the home of J.P. Rose car valeting services. The new Broken Cross school was built on the Weston Estate on Parkett Heyes Road. It generated so much traffic that it was deemed necessary to make the road one way.

We have a special school in Park Lane for those who are less fortunate, alongside the

College of Further Education. The College moved to the new site from its original place on Park Green to the rear of what was the Town's library.

There is a private school on Beech Lane, a smaller version of the Kings, with only paying pupils, all very smart in their uniforms. I once had the pleasure of transporting their cricket team to Stoneyhurst school in the Ribble Valley and frequently took their fencing team to away matches. Alas, I fear that this lovely old house is now in imminent danger of demolition to make way for houses, if the school can find alternative land to build a new building.

Schools we have lost include Christ Church, St. Andrews, Central School (now St. Barnabas) and Mill Street, which was actually entered from Pickford Street; St. George's and Hurdsfield next to their respective churches.

One which will have fond memories for many is that of Duke Street. It stood opposite the Regal Cinema and was built about 1813. It closed around April 1966 to become yet another car park. Many will also remember St. Albans with its small playground to the rear, now also a car park. This school was moved to Priory Lane near to the Leisure Centre, causing much traffic congestion when the mothers drive to pick up their charges.

One of the smaller schools lost to demolition was that of Beech Lane School. It was not actually on Beech Lane but in Justice Street tucked away between Fowler Street and Spring Gardens. This area is not well frequented now since most of the access routes to it have been closed off by the Council in the interest of better traffic flow. The school was probably ripe for demolition as my memory is of a very small yard with outside toilets. I have no doubt that the staff and pupils would have been pleased to move to a new building even if it was a happy school with lots of good memories for the pupils who went there.

One school I cannot remember with pupils although I suspect it must have had is that in Windmill Street next to St. Peters Church. The building, now converted to living accommodation, has an inscription over it which reads 'War Memorial Hall 1914-19'.

As a pupil of the Kings School I well remember my trips to both the High School and Central School in pursuit of female company. I was often reprimanded by the female heads for hanging around the school gates during dinner breaks. Surely I was not the only one?

Whilst I feel most privileged to have attended the Kings School and gained a good education, I actually disliked school and often used to wonder why people say that school days are the happiest days of your life. The only things I enjoyed at school were school dinners and cricket. In my case it was school holidays that were the happiest days of my life. They were never long enough for me. This led me to supplement them by taking additional days off during term time on a fairly regular basis. The teachers tried hard to instil into me the school curriculum but I only really worked hard at art and metal work. Out of a class of thirty two boys the competition to be regularly below the thirty mark seemed to be mainly between myself and David Bayley. Never the less both of us seemed to have done well for ourselves in our working lives.

The teachers I remember, some sadly deceased, were T.T. Shaw (Chimp), Headmaster; Mr Harvey Deputy Head; Slimy Miller, Bursar; Bum Jones, art; Norman Jardine, metalwork; Smith, woodwork; D.H. Burt, English literature and Rambling Club; Johnny Yomans Rushbrook, maths; Slogger Logan, cricket; A.D. Siddal, P.T. or P.E. as it is called now; Dickie Haresine and Inky Waterman. Other names escape me for the moment.

I left Kings in about 1952 so I could not have been a suspect when the school's main hall was gutted by fire in October 1960. I was guilty of many misdemeanours during my stay at the school as other former pupils will testify, but arson was not one of them.

There are other schools who were an unknown quantity to me but a mention may jog the memory of some others. The Old Modern School in Great King Street was built in 1844 but during my early childhood was a school clinic. We were regularly marched there to have our teeth inspected and the lice removed from our heads by the nit nurse. It also dispensed cod liver oil and orange juice to those who needed them, and most of us did after the end of the Second World War. The thought makes me feel very old. The Modern School, as it was known, amalgamated with the Grammar School in 1910. One of the current occupants of the building is Silk F.M. or Radio Macclesfield as it is often called. The building has seen much history and I hope will continue to do so if it can survive the pressure of those who prefer demolition as the first option.

There was an old school known as London Road School of which I know very little other than the fact that it went along with all the cottages around it and was in the area of White Street. It must have had pupils; were you one of them? I only recall its demise.

The Industrial School was in Brook Street, built in 1866 at a cost of £3000. The building still stands but is no longer a school. I often wonder what it was they taught. I can only imagine that it might have been some sort of college of further education or perhaps a training school for apprentices. Something for you to think about.

Our hospitals like our schools have an interesting history. As I understand it the West Park Hospital, formerly accessed via Prestbury Road, was built to house the poor people of the town who had no work and therefore no place to live. It was the workhouse and only later became a hospital when the need for a workhouse ceased. The term workhouse conjures up thoughts of Dickens and Oliver Twist but whilst life there would not have been a bed of roses I do believe the building was a gesture by the rich people of the town to do something for those less fortunate than themslves.

The Infirmary is a different matter. This was built with money donated by the population of the Town in a public subscription and only later changed hands in 1948 with the creation of the National Health Service. The NHS took over the running of the Town's hospital and I presume the ownership of the building under the twenty year rule. They, as is well known, sold the building. It was not really theirs to sell in the first place but Sainsburys got it for another supermarket! The local council made a gesture on behalf of the public by refusing planning permission for a supermarket, but when faced by the threat from the National Health Service, that the proposed new hospital might not come to Macclesfield, they caved in. They offered only token resistance at the appeal to the Department of the Environment.

To make the matter worse, Sainsburys offered to pay for the new road layout, with a new roundabout on the Prestbury Road, so long as access to the town via Prestbury Road was cut off. Macclesfield agreed to this, so all traffic was funnelled past the new superstore despite the stupidity of directing all traffic from Alderley and Prestbury on a detour to get to the main car park at Whalley Heys.

The Council argued that the area was not large enough to accommodate a four exit roundabout on Prestbury Road, at its junction with Cumberland Street. The new roundabout appeared as if by magic almost overnight. A 'fait acomplit'. The Council were brought before the ombudsman for maladministration and not only found guilty but severely reprimanded. The had not gone through the proper procedures of consultation. Unfortunately the ombudsman has no powers when faced with a determined council so its findings were just ignored and Lord Sainsbury got what he wanted. That was the way it

St. George's School, High Street, built 1835.

Catholic School, Chester Road.

St. Peter's School, Windmill Street.

The Old Modern School, Great King Street, 1844.

was seen by many of us at the time. A good example of what money can buy you.

I also seem to remember that one of the planning conditions was that the stone in the Infirmary was to be used in the construction of the new supermarket. It was my view at the time that this did not happen. Some of the beautiful Kerridge Pink stone was used but I believe that most of it was spirited away to build someone a very nice home up in the country. Do you know where all that lovely stone ended up?

My other memories of the Infirmary are of helping Dr Bordo and Mr Proctor, of the Boy Scout Movement, to decorate the children's ward for Christmas, and, later, visits to the nurses' home just below it on Westminster Road for a brief period when courting a young Irish student nurse.

On Moss Lane stands a building, now an old peoples' home, called Weston Park Nursing Care Centre. It was once the Isolation Hospital. When it was built it was in the middle of the countryside and well away from the town. It is soon, regrettably, to be swallowed up by more houses and light industrial units. I did spend some time there as a child but am not sure of my illness, probably scarlet fever. I am grateful to the hospital for my living as long as I have. I suspect I might have died but for the care they gave me.

The Town now has a large new hospital on Victoria Road along with a number of private hospitals. It has recently been threatened with the loss of its accident and emergency ward. Despite the huge hospital car park, staff still park on Victoria Road, both day and night.

I have left the largest hospital until the last as I have many happy memories of working there as a wages clerk for three and a half years. Parkside was comprised of a number of Victorian buildings in spacious grounds. It was built as an asylum and as such was surrounded on all sides by eight foot high corrugated iron fencing to keep the inmates in. The high fences, making the whole area secret, gradually came down after the War as the treatment of patients changed from straight jackets to drugs, and patients were treated rather than just restrained.

The hospital had its own laundry, fire engine, printers' shop, coach, nurses' home, gardeners, and a farm. In all it was like a self sufficient little town isolated from the outside world. I worked there from about 1957 after finishing my national service as a fireman in the Royal Air Force. I loved every minute of my time there. After I left they sold off the farm for building land as the demand for houses increased.

Later the Main Hall, where as treasurer of the social club I had organised many a dance with famous bands, was destroyed by fire, never to be rebuilt. The hospital is now suffering the final indignity of having many of its beautiful buildings destroyed for more of those Jones houses or 'desirable residences'.

My three and a half years in the wages office alongside Albert Wrigley, Geoff Bennett and Dick Hankinson were wonderful years in which I met with all the staff every Thursday on the occasion of wage packet distribution. During my time a computer of sorts was introduced which necessitated another member of staff in the wages department. No cost saving there!

I could tell many stories about that period of my life at Parkside Hospital but I will tell just one about a patient who worked in the social centre kitchens where I regularly had my lunch. The patient was Alf Bray; I think he was around the age of sixty having been resident in the hospital since the age of sixteen. He was almost always missing from his duties on a Wednesday afternoon. It was later discovered that he used to borrow a handcart and attend Brocklehursts salerooms to ply for trade as a delivery source to those who had purchased heavy or bulky furniture, to boost his meagre hospital pocket money allowance.

When he was found out he was discharged from the hospital and found residence in Coronation Street. He later cut his front door in half so he could look out onto the street with only the top half of the door open, as in a stable door. Some of you may well remember seeing him in the Town centre, sometimes carrying a sandwich board advertising for a local shop, but more often he would parade the streets carrying his large base drum and playing, very badly, a bugle, to the amusement of the crowds.

Government policy of care in the community, right or wrong, has lead to this once beautiful area of Macclesfield being sacrificed for more houses. I expect that hundreds of staff and inmates will mourn its passing. Many have many happy memories. My most lasting are of being treasurer of the social club and of playing for the hospital cricket team.

If only we could go back and do it all again, I wonder if we would do it differently. Only time will tell if we got it right. I suspect we did not. Maybe it is just a fact of life that money and big business rules and individual's feelings count for nothing today. I do not want to return to Victorian values but the pendulum has swung so far the other way and it distresses me to see the wholesale destruction of a beautiful township just so Jones Homes can build on more of our green and pleasant land.

Old London Road School.

Industrial School, Brook Street.

Bridge over Victoria Road connecting the hospital at Parkside with its farm. Demolished 1980.

Old Regal Cinema, Duke Street.

Drome Cinema, Chestergate, corner of Catherine Street.

CHAPTER FIVE
PICTURE HOUSES & DANCE HALLS

Macclesfield used to have five picture houses and one opera house but today none of them exist, and although we are promised a new multi-screen cinema, after two years of waiting nothing has got beyond the planning stage. The population of Macclesfield must travel to Stockport or Manchester to see a film on the big screen.

In thinking about the demise of the silver screen in our town I will start with the Premier as it was the closest to where I lived around 1947/48. The Premier picture house was in Vincent Street on the corner of Hobson Street and opposite Hyde's garage, which proudly possessed a petrol pump at the side of the footpath. Behind the cinema was a large house in its own grounds surrounded by a thick shrubbery largely of rhododendron.

As with most of the cinemas the programme changed twice a week and most had two showings of the programme in the evenings Mondays to Saturdays and afternoon matinees on Wednesdays and Saturdays. There was at that time no films shown on a Sunday, that came later when attendances slumped with the spread of television broadcasts.

At one point in my life I was a regular attender at the Saturday morning shows at the Premier especially for children. Every Saturday morning gave us an exciting episode of Flash Gordon, an early spaceman, long before Dr Who appeared or space travel became real. Each week would end at a critical point, as with Dick Barton on the radio, ensuring our attendance the next week.

In addition to the serial there was always a cowboy film or just occasionally it might be Tarzan, Lord of the Jungle, or Lassie the Dog who always averted danger in the nick of time. My favourite was Johnny Mack Brown who dressed in white as he was the goodie, to distinguish him from the baddie who was usually dressed in black. The children would cheer the goodie and boo the baddie, or sometimes it would be Indians who were booed and they were recognised by the wearing of feathers. Other cowboys of the era were Hopalong Cassidy, Gene Autry, and Roy Rogers with his horse Trigger. The Lone Ranger and Tonto came along much later. We always left the cinema riding up the street on an imaginary horse pretending to be the cowboy of the film and shouting "bang bang, you're dead", to the usual reply "no you missed me, I got you first."

I think we paid nine old pence, or if we were happy to use the side entrance and sit on the wooden seats of the first two rows we paid only three old pence.

As television became more widespread the popularity of the big screen declined and soon the Premier was to close to become a car showroom for Hyde's garage. It was later demolished and replaced by the back wall of the new B & Q superstore.

Another picture palace to fall at an early stage was the Cinema off Buxton Road which you would know if you lived around the Victoria Park area. I cannot honestly say I know much about the cinema as I only went there once in my life. My memory is of a very uninviting building something like an aircraft hanger. I think it may have had a tin roof as when it rained you could hear it while watching the film. Maybe I am being a little unfair after only one visit nearly fifty years ago!

What is certain is that after its last performance it was used as a shop for the building trade. It was later demolished to make way for the widening of Buxton Road at its junction with Commercial Road just below Arthur Watling's motorcycle shop and the Bull Inn. These road improvements did not seem to stop runaway lorries running into S and M supplies on a regular basis.

The third cinema we lost was the Regal in Duke Street affectionately known as "the bug hut". The building stood just opposite the Duke Street School and after closing it was used as a night club, which opened and closed on several occasions for various reasons. Up until recently the building was held together with steel ties, looking very much as if it would fall down before it could be demolished. When I last looked at the building it had been renovated outside and had a board advertising the building to let for leisure facilities.

The old Regal was run by a husband and wife team. She sold the tickets at the box office and then met you inside and took the ticket she had just sold you and showed you to your seat. She also sold the ice creams in the interval. Her husband operated the projector which was positioned so low that those in the back row could and often did make shadows on the screen with their hands or with their heads, if they came and went during the performance. This always raised hoots of derision from the audience. Sometimes the film would break and you could see the film, stuck in the gate of the projector, visibly melt and smoke on the screen. The audience would become very vocal whilst the film was spliced and rethreaded through the projector. They would show their disgust by slow handclaps or stamping feet in unison. Sometimes they would start to sing "why are we waiting" and occasional obscenities were heard, but in general it was all good humoured banter.

The Picture Dome in Chestergate was a little more upper class, they had a commissionaire standing at the entrance. It was his job to open the doors for customers and to marshall the queues outside. He would strut up and down looking important in his red uniform just like a sergeant major. Despite this class it was also destined to close and was replaced by bingo which was the up and coming entertainment as whist and beetle drives lost their following. The future of the building became in doubt when after thirty one years as a bingo hall it closed down and became a target for bill posting. It is currently being renovated, having a floor put in to make it two storey and will be given a new lease of life as a warehouse and office complex.

The last of the cinemas to close was the Majestic which stood next to the Salvation Army Citadel in Mill Street until that moved to make way for a shopping precinct. This cinema was the tops, showing all the best films and with a large staff, with the two commissionaires wearing dinner jackets and bow ties. It also had a small restaurant upstairs for those who could afford to take seats upstairs. The Majestic was built by the Higginbotham family and run by them throughout its life. It was used almost every year for a pantomime at Christmas time. I wonder what happened to all those who appeared every year, in particular the little gentleman who stood less than four foot six and always got a role. What was his name? Graham Caroll?

In its heyday the Majestic had all the top films but film distribution was not always as it is now. Now we have a new film out and hundreds of copies are made so it can be shown at all the cinemas at the same time and tie in to TV advertising. When 'Gone with the Wind' and 'South Pacific' came out they were both shown in Manchester at the Gaumont for two years before they got to Macclesfield.

Alas even the Majestic has succumbed to closure and the latest news is that it is to become a pub and this even before we have a replacement multi screen. It seems sad that even though the Majestic was still a viable business no one wanted to take it on when Mr. Higginbotham retired.

Macclesfield used to have its own theatre in Catherine Street which was called the Opera House, until it burnt down. I do not actually remember it but I do recall seeing the burnt out shell which stood derelict for many years behind the closed iron gates. It was a

Majestic Cinema, Mill Street. Next to Salvation Army Citadel.

Stanley Hall entrance, Castle Street, flanked by Wellings Optician.

Drill Hall clock tower in Bridge Street following the demolition of the rest of the building.

shame it was never rebuilt; was it lack of an insurance pay out or just poor attendance making the project no longer viable? Did you ever see a live performance there; it was to the rear of the drill hall? I think MADS could have made good use of it.

The town had a large number of dance halls which in addition to their primary function were used frequently for other social activities. The Town Hall had a beautiful function room at the head of the impressive staircase. All dances were ticket only and many insisted on formal evening dress - you had to be someone to get a ticket. I only attended one dance there and that was the Civil Defence Ball, of which organisation I was at the time the treasurer. The club had their own small premises in Birch House which still stands in Bridge Street on the corner of Waterloo Street West. The use of the Town Hall for dances decreased over the years until it came down almost to just the Lord Mayor's annual bash. Even this event ceased when the room was taken over as office accommodation to house the computer staff needed when we were introduced to first the poll tax and then the community charge.

The second most popular hall for dancing was the Stanley Hall in Castle Street which at one point had dances weekly. They were very popular with ballroom dancers. Dancing was not a thing I was good at so I did not go very often. I did however appear once outside the Stanley Hall playing a drum to attract attention to a bazaar being staged by St. John's church, probably Christmas 1959.

Another popular venue was the Liberal club in Queen Victoria Street; its proper title was the Brocklehurst Memorial Hall. During my youth it was called the El Rio and boasted amongst its entertainers the Beatles before they were world famous. The building was also used as a snooker and billiards hall and was the home of the Adelphi Players whose most famous member was Jean Alexander. She won fame as Hilda Ogden in Coronation Street. Eventually use of the building waned, so like many others a consortium of business men purchased the site and eventually got permission to turn it into - yes you've guessed it - another supermarket and car park.

The Drill Hall in Bridge Street was another venue used for dancing and charity bazaars although it was built as a military barracks and housed the local Territorial Army, part of the Cheshire Regiment. This later moved to new premises next to the new fire station, and is now another building scheduled for redundancy following government withdrawal of funds to support army reserves. You may well have been a member of the T. A. and you will remember Ernie Foden who I think was colour sergeant. He later became a bailiff for the county court. Another name closely connected for many years was a cobbler from 18 Cross Street by the name of Danny Norton who was the band master.

When they moved to the new premises, the old building fell into disrepair and a local business man had plans approved for conversion to flats. So the whole building was demolished in 1999 apart from the square tower, a familiar site to Maxonions.

A hall with which I had a long association is the Morton Jubilee Hall on Union Road. Mr Morton had the hall built in 1939 as a social centre for the employees of the Hovis factory, so I was told. It was Mr. Morton's wish that the hall be made available free of charge to any charitable organisation who wished to use it for fundraising events. I wonder therefore how it is that Cheshire County Council seem to have got their hands on the property and the provision made by Mr Morton seems to no longer exist.

The building has extensive rooms on the ground floor used as snooker and table tennis rooms, along with dressing rooms in connection with the hall above. The hall had a good seating capacity and a self contained kitchen and during my time at St. John's I made use of the facilities. I well recall playing Old King Cole in a pantomime where the scouts got together with the Patterson Starlets. I also had need to use the building for discos during my term as president of the Macclesfield and District Riding Club. Alas the use by youth organisations in later years, under the control of the Cheshire County Council, seemed poorly organised as complaints by neighbours about noise, fights and under age drinking caused a decline in the use of this valuable venue.

St. Michael's Parish Rooms were very popular for small dances and socials. It was always referred to as the Tin Tab (short for tabernacle) although I am assured it was never a place of worship for the Jewish faith. I am not entirely sure how it met its end, I suspect it caught fire as it was all wood and corrugated iron, but I may be wrong; it could have just fallen into disrepair and been demolished.

There was a similar building in Jordongate known as Martinue Hall. I don't know where the name came from. It was used for beetle drives and social events on a regular basis being close to the wooden hut occupied by the Parish Church scout group on land now the site of the postal sorting office. If you do not know what a beetle drive is, it is something similar to a whist drive - I suggest you ask your granny. Like many other halls made of wood it has been replaced with yet another car park.

Most churches had their own halls near to the church and held social events at times like Valentines day, Halloween, Bonfire night, and Christmas. One I will always remember is that of Hurdsfield School next to the church, Lansdown Street, now a site for houses, for it is here I learned Scottish country dancing.

The main hall at King's School, before the great fire, held dances and had a flourishing film club showing films on a Friday night to members.

The Heritage Centre on Roe Street, formerly known as the Large Sunday School, has a hall upstairs used now for concerts. Built in 1813 by voluntary contribution, there is a monument outside as a tribute to the founder John Whittaker, dated 6th May 1846.

The Sunday School in Lord Street, home of the MADS, had a period, I think between 1945 and 1950, when it housed the public library whilst dry rot in the Town's library was removed. The library did briefly return to its old building but later moved to the corner of Brunswick Street in the shell of an old bank building - the Manchester and Liverpool District Bank built 1881. It was intended that the old bank should be demolished and rebuilt but public opposition to the loss of yet another architectural feature forced a rethink.

The Lord Street Sunday School is now the permanent home of the Amateur Dramatic Society. Their hard work and determination paid off and the group and the building now flourish - and will I trust for years to come. Apart from the parking problem I suspect they are very happy in their venue, although if you were to find a better theatre for their productions I am sure this building would quickly be demolished.

Despite the loss of so many halls, due to idle citizens who prefers to watch TV and drink lager from supermarket cans, the Town has managed to build at least two new halls. The senior citizens hall on the corner of the Duke Street car park survived demolition shortly after it was built when the line of Churchill Way threatened it. Somehow a compromise was reached and the new road was curved around the new hall, only restricting access to the rear entrance behind the stage. I had occasions to hire the hall mostly for the annual prize giving of the Riding Club. This hall replaced the one lost in Derby Street. The other new hall is Heys Hall on Weston Estate. It has had a variety of uses; the one I remember most is its regular use for jumble sales. Despite its siting near to the old persons' bungalows it has been a target of vandals for many years, but it still survives.

Heritage Centre, Roe Street.

Morton Jubilee Hall, Union Road.

Senior Citizens' Hall, Derby Street.

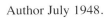

Author July 1948.

Sir Robert Peel pub, now a private house.

CHAPTER SIX
LIVING IN BARTON STREET

In 1948, when the state of Israel was created and the NHS was formed, I was a schoolboy living at 193 Park Lane. Our back garden ran through the block into Barton Street, the lower end. I hardly ever used the front door of the house because my bicycle was kept in a shed in the garden, and I always considered myself a Barton Street kid and a member of the gang.

In those days the street was cobbled and there were no parked cars; in fact I think we were the first to have a motor car. We purchased a very old secondhand Standard with a truck body and a canvas hood which proved ideal for me and my mates when the weather was inclement. I must have spent many hours in the back of that truck.

Returning recently to the street I was really suprised to see it blocked with parked cars on both sides as far as the eye could see. It was not easy to visualise the street we played football and cricket in when the only thing to stop play was the arrival of the milkman's horse or the man who came to empty the pig bin. For those who do not recall this, most areas had their pig bin. This was proper recycling - everyone put their potato peelings, bread crusts and assorted stale food into them and it was collected regularly and fed to pigs on a local farm.

It made me realise that almost all of Society's problems today stem from the introduction of the motor car which was inevitably followed by the supermarket and then out of town shopping. All this mobility has been both an advantage and a curse. Maybe it was a retrograde step. We had a bus stop outside our front door and the North Western Road Car Co. put on an hourly service to Crewe via Congleton and Sandbach, plus three buses per hour to all parts of the Town. There was no shortage of public transport so no one really needed a car.

Almost everything we needed was within two minutes walk of home. I'll try to explain. I lived next door to doctor's surgeries on both sides with Drs Gillies, Mark, Heart, Varley, and Tannebaum. On Park Lane at its junction with South Park Road we had a dentist, and the shop on the corner of Brown Street dispensed drugs on prescription. We had the Premier Cinema in Vincent Street, and pubs galore; the Park Tavern in Park Lane; the Prince Albert in Newton Street; the Sir Robert Peel opposite the Newtown Methodist Church in South Park Road (later to become a shop selling tropical fish). Potts lighting shop in Park Lane used to be the Stag and Pheasant.

There was plenty of employment in the factories in Vincent Street and the factory in Brown Street. We were privileged to have the labour exchange on our doorstep in South Park Road, now replaced by a town centre shop. In addition to the Methodist Chapel we had the lovely Church of St. John's in Statham Street. There was scouts, cubs, guides, brownies and local amateur dramatics in the school room of St John's, now Mafeking Hall.

The South Park gave us fishing, tennis, roller skating, bowls, pitch and putt golf, swings and roundabouts; and in the summer live music from brass bands. The park also provided a venue for a children's day nursery. About the only thing not within the two minutes walk was the school in Athey Street or in my case the Kings School about twelve minutes walking away or three minutes on my bicycle.

We had the off licence in Brown Street at number 60, on the corner of Buckley Street, now called the Crown liqueur store. We had two chip chops, one in Brown Street, who sold the best mushy peas, served in your own bowl, and Molly Torson's in Crossall Street, who opened almost every day at lunchtime and most evenings until well into the night.

We had two photographers, Mr Kirk who lived with his sister at 45 Barton Street and had a shop at 47, and there was the well known Charlie Berrisford who lived in Park Lane in one of the houses known as the Twelve Apostles.

Barton Street had its own monumental masons, by the name of Gorton and Kellett I believe. I used to sit and watch these two men chisel away at large pieces of stone just to make lasting tributes to the deceased; it was truly fascinating.

There were many other services. Mr Davies the cobbler at 86 Brown Street; a painter and decorator's shop at number 67; in Park Lane a hairdressers at 173; and across the road Palin's shop with its own bakery at the rear of the shop (at present empty but has been recently an outlet for sofas and chairs). We even had a British Road Services parcel depot in Newton Street, now Macclesfield Motor Factors, run by Bert Riley and family.

We were privileged to have a grocers at 44 Barton Street where you could buy most anything. The bread was not sliced or even wrapped apart from a piece of tissue paper. Sugar came in blue paper bags tied up with string, and biscuits were sold loose in pounds or ounces - now illegal as you can now only buy in grams; a case of a government gone mad! Imagine being prosecuted for buying a pound of potatoes.

At the bottom of the street we had Mrs Place's shop who sold items like paraffin, firelighting, (sticks I mean) and gas mantles. The shop on the corner of Brown Street and Park Lane also sold groceries and doubled as a pharmacy and post office, conveniently placed behind the post box on Park Lane.

The new pharmacy at number 209 Park Lane was I think at one time a bakery and more recently I think a shop selling soft furnishings. At 156 Park Lane there is a butcher's shop which still survives today. Selling meat since before the Second World War, it was started by a Mr Millward and then for many years run by a Mr Read. Across the road was Robins' TV and Aerials, which used to be Ferrars Gents' Outfitters. I recall looking longingly into the shop window at a black shirt with embroidery on it, which I could not afford to buy, in the days of drainpipe trousers and suede shoes.

My friends in Barton Street, from the bottom, were, at number 3 Roland Smith, who was to become landlord of the Three Pigeons public house, and at number 17, John Hough who became a top class football referee. We once played for the same football team. He had a younger sister. At number 19 was David Ashness who worked for post office telephones and had two older sisters, Joan and Marion. Then there was Mrs Conway at 21 and Mrs Simpson as 23. At number 27 was Robert Lockett and his younger brother Graham; their mother was Welsh and their father was a wagon repairer on the railway. At number 29 was Gordon Lennard, a little older than the rest of us. On the other side of the street was Graham Jones at number 42 and Roy Evett at number 26. Sorry if I missed anyone!

Getting back to the facilities we enjoyed; there was a shop which was a very popular haunt for me on the corner of Park Lane and Park Vale Road. We had to pass it each time we went to the Park, several times a day. When I say pass it, most times we would stop and buy ice cream or sweets and if we could afford it minerals in glass bottles with two pence back on the returned empty. The shop, called Morgan's, was run by a little man and his wife. He at one stage opened his front room as a tea room for little old ladies returning from the bowling greens. It later changed hands and was run by two men and they called the shop Jonty's. The shop has now gone and is converted to an office block under the name of Festival House.

One particular shop has special memories for me, that of Billy Lennard, newsagents at the bottom of our street. I worked paper rounds for Mr Lennard, morning, evening and two rounds on Sundays for a total of twelve shillings and sixpence per week. For that I had to also go to the station at Hibel Road and collect the evening papers on a very heavy shop bike with a carrier on the front. Whilst we waited for the papers to arrive the lads would give each other rides on the railway porters' trolleys. The papers would be sorted by Mr Evans, wholesale newsagent, who had a shop on Commercial Road although he actually lived in one of the Twelve Apostles in Park Lane.

I saved my pay as a paper boy and with what I also earned working on the post at Christmas eventually reached my target of £35.5s.0d, the cost of my new bicycle purchased from Shackletons in Churchwallgate. It was a Raleigh Super Lenton in lustre orange and had GB brakes, alloy wheels and Sturmey Archer four speed gears. It was the very latest in cycles and was my pride and joy. We went everywhere together. Unlike children of today whose parents buy them a bike, and after a few days it is flung onto the garage floor and neglected, I was so proud I spent hours cleaning it. I even used to strip down the hubs and clean and grease the ball bearings from time to time. When I went out for a ride and the bike got wet I would clean the bike before I would wash myself and have a meal.

One other job I did whilst a schoolboy was to assist Ernie Bowers the milkman and his horse Major. As the float went up the street I would collect the jugs off window ledges and bring them to the cart where they would be filled from either pint of half pint ladles. I would then return the jug and replace the saucer on the top. On occasions, I remember, the horse would walk on without being told especially where it was treated to the crust off a loaf by a customer.

On a few occasions I was permitted on a Saturday to take the reins and steer the horse as it trotted across Park Green and made for the dairy which was the just off Windmill Street. We would then return to the farm in Moss Lane and I would help feed the pigs and wash the milk churn out ready for the next day. The farm was owned by Staniers of Lyme Green and is now used as offices by effluent services. The tenant farmer's name was Barnes and he had a daughter Diane whom I admired greatly at the time but I never had the courage to tell her so. Girls came rather later in my life.

To return once more to my bike, my most treasured possession. It allowed me to travel. I was used to walking for miles around but the bike got me to other counties. I went as far west as Bangor in Wales and as far south as Ashby de la Zouch in Leicestershire. For a while I also owned a tandem. With my best friend Roy Barton we would go to Middlewich camping, towing a home made four-wheeler trailer.

When I was not out riding my bicycle, I would usually be in the South Park playing tennis or fishing, and it was about this period in my life when I showed an interest in girls. I had had a girlfriend at the age of five but now things became more serious as I found myself spending hours at night in the cycle shed attached to the pavilion in the South Park. With Maria, Diane, Sheila, and Janet, I learnt the art of kissing and breathing at the same time. The timing seemed important to newcomers to this sport.

Those early experiments with girls were of no importance but when I grew older my courting days more often took place on the front bench seat of my MKII Ford Consul in sunburst yellow. But despite this apparent advantage of a flash car I have managed to get through life to date without being taken up the aisle!

When I was fifteen I met a girl who was my first real love. She became more important to me than tennis or fishing! I have never forgotten her. Our relationship was comparatively short and I cannot remember how it ended but I never knew if she felt the same as me. What happened to Olive Massey? Did you know her? Do you have a photograph of her as a teenager? Perhaps she might even read my book.

Alas my recent visit to the South Park was a great disappointment. The shrubbery has all gone, and the flower beds are neglected. The pavilion which burnt down has been replaced by a modern brick structure and is covered in graffiti, dirty and neglected. The old bandstand has lost all its glass doors and looks ready for demolition. I suspect only lack of cash has saved it so far and the last time I saw it trees were growing from its roof.

In my younger days graffiti did exist but it was mostly done with chalk which soon washed away when it rained. The more permanent defacing of property was done with a pen knife in wood and usually involved two sets of initials, a heart and an arrow. Today, with the invention of the felt tip pen and the aerosol paint spray can, the practise appears to be much more prevalent and certainly more lasting on many of our public buildings. The lack of enthusiasm for its removal only seems to give the so called artists tacit approval.

It seems one should never try to go back as nothing is ever as you remember it. You remember only the days when the sun shone and not the days when things went wrong. The good memories outlast the bad ones. Maybe things are better than in my days but when I go back they do not seem to have improved. Perhaps some memories are just illusions?

South Park, New Pavilion.

South Park Pavilion after the fire.

Band Stand, South Park.

George Hotel, Jordongate.

Bull's Head, Broken Cross.

CHAPTER SEVEN
PUBS AND OTHER WATERINGHOLES

Looking around the town I would have thought that Macclesfield had as many public houses per head of population as any town, or more than most. You never have to walk far without coming across a place where you can get your fill of an alcoholic drink. I once read that Stanley Street had twenty-four pubs; many would have been just ale houses of course, and would have been before the introduction of licensing laws.

Whilst we commonly refer to them as pubs they appear in the main to be split into two categories, inns and hotels. I'm not sure of the difference, if there is any. I always thought that a hotel was a place of residence which served drinks and the inn a place where you bought alcohol and sometimes obtained a night's lodging. I think that most of the ones I am about to write about are just the local for the inhabitants of the area. Those on the major roads seem to cater more for passing trade and those who wish to eat out and have a drink with their meal. Many of our local pubs were places where you could play darts or dominoes but times change and our pubs have moved on. They now all seem to provide a pool table, and piped music whether you want it or not.

There was a time when the pubs were supplied by the local brewery, and indeed many pubs brewed their own beer. That was before stricter licensing laws came into force. Macclesfield had two large breweries that I knew of in the days before beer from Bavaria and fizzy lager from Denmark. Even supermarkets now sell a range of beers in 'six packs' favoured by the couch potato who sits all day in front of the TV, a trend which has led to the downfall of some of our local watering holes. I fear more will be lost unless the demand for eating out is filled more by the ale houses than by Macdonalds.

Nowadays our beer comes from places like Burton-on-Trent. We may never again see the horse drawn drey delivering local beers. The firm of Lonsdale and Adshead had a large brewery on Park Green, taken over by Ind Coope. It was later demolished and replaced by an office block, recently itself under threat to make way for more office blocks.

The other big brewery was in Bond Street on the corner of Athey Street. It was called Smiths, or was it Crown brewery, either way it was taken over by Marstons and closed, and now is light industrial units. The demise of our breweries was not the wish of the local consumer but big business dictating to us, based solely on profit margins and not the taste of the product. Those days have gone and with them a loss to the local gardener who would follow the drey horses with bucket and shovel to improve his roses or his rhubarb. I do not think horses will return - at least not until the oil runs out.

Every road into the town is sprinkled with pubs, spaced at regular intervals so the weary traveller could stop and refresh himself every mile or so. I will try to list the places on the approach roads to the Town; most of them still exist. Coming towards Town from the North along Manchester Road we start at The Legh Arms, Adlington; The Ash Tree Inn at Butley, followed by the recently built Brocklehurst Arms at Tytherington and finally The Old Ship Inn on Beech Lane. Entering the town from the east, from Buxton and the Derbyshire Hills, we start with The Cat and Fiddle, said to be the highest pub in England but recently disputed. As we near the edge of the town we have The Setter Dog at Walker Barn and on entering the town close to the canal bridge both The Bridgewater and The Puss in Boots.

Coming from the south along the London Road we start at Bosley with The Queens and The Harrington Arms and closer to the town we have the Fool's Nook on the corner of

Ratcliffe Road. This pub near to the canal was an old coaching house on what was then called Oak Grove and had the name of the Royal Oak, so I believe. Entering the Town boundary we have first the Star Inn followed by the Moss Rose now called The Silkman. I think several attempts to change its name have been made but it will always be known as the Moss Rose after the estate and the bus service. I have never approved of pubs changing their names as many in Macclesfield have done in recent years. These names are local landmarks - you could not give a stranger directions without the use of pub names. The question of landlords not being allowed to change pub names was I believe brought up in the House of Commons by our member of parliament recently.

Entering from the west we have The Blacksmith's Arms, followed by The Cock Inn at Henbury and on the edge of town The Pack Horse hotel at Broken Cross.

There are some minor roads into town such as the one from Bollington, which gives us The Wagon and Horses, and then The Cock and Pheasant. Now we have a new motel on the land where the old Bollington Road crosses the new Silk Road. It goes under the title Middlewood Travel Inn. Strange since it is nowhere near Middlewood and looks more like a theme park than an inn.

If you approach the Town from Rainow down Hurdsfield Road you start with The Highwayman and then in Rainow village The Robin Hood. Closer to the Town you pass The Rising Sun and The George and Dragon. Lower down Hurdsfield Road there is The Three Crowns just below the Ebenezer Chapel, The Britannia just above the post office, and lastly The Flower Pot opposite the church.

From Langley you have the Leather Smithy, the St. Dunston in Langley village, followed by the Church House in Sutton, and where the road goes under the canal the Old King's Head at Gurnett. Finally just before crossing the railway line you find appropriately The Railway View. I am told that there was a pub in Langley called The New Brighton. Did you know it?

If you enter from the hills of Wincle you pass first The Ryles Arms and then The Lamb at Lane Ends, whilst on the Congleton Road you pass the Chain and Gate, The Harrington Arms, The Rising Sun opposite the local tip and finally The Flower Pot at the top of Park Lane. The only other road in is from Alderley when you will pass only The Wizard of the Edge.

As each housing estate was built around the town a new pub was built to satisfy the needs of the residents. On the Hurdsfield estate they built The Mulberry Bush and the Woodman to replace those lost when they cleared the area to make way for the new flats along side the Victoria Park. The Weston estate was provided for with the Weston Pub and the Ivy Leaf, whilst Upton Priory got the Oval.

It seems that when they built the Moss Estate it was not thought necessary to build them a new pub as The Moss Rose and The Golden Lion both on Moss Lane would be thought sufficient for the needs of the new tenants. A new pub was built on the new settlement around Thornton Square and this was called The Weaver.

All the others I can recall are: The Albion, 6 London Road, The Three Crowns, Mill Green, The George Hotel, 48 Jordongate. On Waters Green near the Central Station we have The Queen's Hotel, The Old Millstone, The Nag's Head, The Watersgreen Tavern, and The Bull and Gate, which is now called The '108s' after the steps behind it. In Sunderland Street we have The George and Dragon and The Jolly Sailor, whilst round the corner in Brook Street we have The Wharf and The Commercial renamed The Boarhound. Hurdsfield Road has The Durham Ox; Roe Street, The Prince of Wales; and Coare Street,

The British Flag. Crompton Road has The Bruce Arms, The Crompton Road Tavern and The Crofton Hotel. Little Street has The Three Pigeons; Windmill Street, The Dolphin; and round the corner in Black Road we have both The Navigation and The Beehive.

In Oxford Road we have the Oxford now spelt The Ox fford. Prestbury Road has The Plough; Steeple Street, The Franklin; Bond Street, The Crown; and down Backwallgate is an old pub called The Castle. At Pickford Street we had another Royal Oak but since I started writing the book it appears to have changed to 'Aborigines cafe and bar'.

We have The Park Tavern and The Ivy House in Park Lane and The Bull's Head at Broken Cross. In Station Street, where we used to have a railway station, is The Plough, whilst in Chester Road there is The Chester Road Tavern on the corner of Anderson Street. The Royal Oak in King Edward Street has been renamed and is called Maxwell's. The Red Lion in Catherine Street changed its name to The Barnfield, I cannot think why, and The Bear's Head in Mill Street has become The Filigree and Firkin.

Chestergate currently has three pubs. The Bate Hall has a long history which is displayed on a board in the pub lounge for all to read. The pub first appeared in 1525 although there is some evidence that an ale house may have existed on the site even before that date. The name could well be derived from the fact that bear baiting and cock fighting took place in the yard to the rear. There are stories about highwaymen and ghosts and the premises has a priest hole where clergy would be hidden when Henry the Eighth turned up.

There are two pubs on the corner of Little Street, one The Old King's Head and the other renamed The Amsterdam. Many of you will remember it as The Swan with Two Necks. This is not a reference to a mythical bird but a corruption of the name Swan with two nicks. This refers to the practise of cutting notches in the beaks of swans to identify those which the crown claimed ownership of. In years gone by it was quite normal for a monarch to have as the centrepiece to his banquet a large swan.

The last few I can remember are The Traveller's Rest in Cross Street, The Sun on Mill Lane, The Evening Star in James Street, on the corner of John Street, The Peel's Arms in Peel Street, on the corner of Cholmondly Street, The Lord Byron in St George's Street, on the corner of Chapel Street, The Fox and Grapes in Pitt Street, on the corner of Byron Street, The White Swan in Rodney Street, The White Lion on Mill Street, on the corner of Duke Street, The Baths Hotel on Green Street, to the rear of the old baths, the Hole i'th' Wall (my favourite name), regrettably changed to The Blueberry, and The Brewer's Arms in Bridge Street.

Now I will list the ones that we have lost starting with those which have closed but are still standing. An obvious one is the Macclesfield Arms on Jordongate, a fine building indeed. The Bluebell in Mill Lane, and the Orange Tree in Mill Lane, where the World's heaviest man lived until his demise, when it was necessary to have a window removed to get his coffin in and out of the building - much has already been written about Leo Witton, Canadian by birth. The Pig and Whistle in Mill Street was for years Marshall Carr's electrical shop, and it recently reverted to a pub only to close again. Bridge House was a pub and stands in Brook Street at the corner of Maydews Passage. The Sir Robert Peel in South Park Road changed to a shop selling tropical fish and is now a private house. The Butcher's Arms in Chester Road near to the junction with Chestergate has its original windows, with the pub name etched into the glass. The Wine Vaults is on the junction of Mill Street and Castle Street, and one you may not remember, The Volunteer, was on the corner of Charlotte Street West and Church Street West. Another Albion on Bridge Street is now an office block. The Roe Street Tavern was between Bridge and Water Streets.

16th Century Bate Hall, Chestergate.

Bate Hall Yard to the rear of the pub.

Hole i'th' Wall, Old Park Lane.

Macclesfield Arms.

Orange Tree Inn, Mill Lane.

The Pig and Whistle, Mill Street.

Now for those pubs which have been demolished and will never be seen again. I will start with a pub I never knew The Seven Stars in Old Mill Lane, replaced by the Seven Stars Garage. The Bluebell in Manchester Road looked much like an old farmhouse and maybe was; it was always a recognised bus stop just opposite the new Brocklehurst Arms. The Railway Hotel stood on Hibel Road directly opposite the entrance to Hibel Road station. The Park Hotel caught fire and was later demolished to make way for a new road. The same new road saw the end of The Talbot Hotel on Chester Road.

I seem to recall a Pack Horse Hotel on Jordongate but it is not there now. It think it was demolished to make way for the new library building. Calamine Square lost Ye Old Rose Inn, a favourite haunt of both Fred Lomas and Arthur Elkin who were in the coaching business. It was said that the Rose only served Adshead's mild beer.

Brunswick Street lost The Feathers, a pub with a somewhat unsavoury reputation, ironically knocked down to make way for the new police station. Chestergate lost The Derby Arms - not in Derby Street - whose name can still be seen in the old plaster of the shop now called Blush Lingerie. The Spread Eagle stood on the corner of Westminster Street and Chestergate but I cannot remember it myself. At 53 Chestergate, lost to the inner relief road, was The Flying Horse, which I understand closed as a coaching inn about 1919.

Mill Street lost The Green Dragon at number 47 a long time ago . It was somewhere near Waterstones bookshop. It would have been very distinctive as it had a tree growing through the centre of the pub, out through the roof. Roe Street lost the White Hart when the road from the dams steps was closed and built over by Sutton Engineering.

In Union Street there was a pub called The Union and I am told that there was a Berrisfords on Mill Street, at the top of Backwallgate where Mothercare now stands. On Buxton Road, on the corner of Davenport Street stood a very impressive building known as The Royal Oak. It was later to become the spares department for Gleave Motors. The building was lost about the time they built the new flats at Victoria Park. When this development took place they demolished and replaced The Woodman. The Fence Tavern and The Waterloo were not replaced. Neither were The Royal Oak in Commercial Road or the Elephant and Castle. The Elephant and Castle did have its license transferred to a new pub on the Hurdsfield Estate called the Mulberry Bush but regrettably the licensee died two days before the move was to have taken place. Some time later they demolished The Bull on Buxton Road and built a new pub with the same name as part of the new flats complex.

There was a pub called The Three Townships which stood close to the old railway bridge over Hurdsfield Road and next to the River Bollin. Up to the time of its demolition to make way for the new Silk road it was used as offices for Carswells Parcels.

I have left until the last the one which really started the rot. The Angel in the Market Place was a beautiful building and did not merit demolition. At the time the Council was at the start of an orgy of unnecessary rape of the Town's architecture. In their opinion new was better and the wishes of the population counted for nothing. It took many years for the public to raise their voices loud enough to be heard. Now the Council and its officers think very carefully before embarking on such drastic actions. In the past those that cared did not have a voice but now a number of action groups police Council decisions.

There were other places one could drink. There were working men's clubs and snooker halls such as the British Legion, Broken Cross Club and The Trades Hall in Chatham Street and the Sportsman in Chestergate previously used as a dancing school. The Town also has its guest houses and large hotels like The Belgrade and The Mottram Hall to name but two.

The Wine Vaults, Castle Street.

Railway Hotel, Hibel Road.

Park Hotel, Prestbury Road.

Flying Horse Inn, a coaching inn in Chestergate.

White Hart, Roe Street, demolished 1984.

The Three Townships.

Whilst I was the president of Macclesfield and District Riding Club we used The Flower Pot on Congleton Road and The Queen's Hotel for many of our monthly meetings. During my twenty eight years in the coach business our annual Christmas celebration for the drivers was held at various pubs. Those that come to mind are The Commercial, The Queen's at Bosley, The George, when Ray Naden was landlord, The Sun at Rainow, and more recently The George and Dragon at Higher Hurdsfield.

In addition to serving alcohol, pubs provide an essential service to the public as meeting places. There is darts, cribbage, skittles, and more recently pool and piped music, bar snacks and even evening meals. But many of our pubs have not survived and I fear many more will go. I for one would like to see the local bars revived with more local beers.

I am much indebted to John Crawford, who had been before his retirement the licensee of The Waterloo, The Evening Star, The Railway View, and The Star Inn. He has helped me with much of my information and has given me a list of the public houses for the year 1910. Although Macclesfield has increased in size considerably since that date the number of public houses has fallen dramatically. The list shows 157 in Macclesfield itself and that was before the estates were built. My list of those today, including on the roads entering the town only amounts to 96, plus 14 that I know have closed but still stand and 22 that I recall being demolished. I will list all those on the 1910 list that have not already been mentioned previously in this chapter.

Albert Inn, 43 Mill Street, American Tavern, 43 Brown Street, Beech Park Tavern, 130 Beech Lane, Bird in Hand, 15 Commercial Road, Black's Head, 17 Mill Street, Blacksmith's Arms, 168 Buxton Road, Borough Arms, Unicorn Gateway, Boundry Tavern, 17 Eastgate, Bowling Green Inn, Cuckstoolpit Hill, British Columbia, 2 Crossall Street, Brown Jug, 81 Park Lane, Brunts Vaults, 63 Mill Street, Brunswick Hotel, 16 Hibel Road, Bull and Gate, Chestergate, Crown and Anchor, Stanley Street, Dog and Partridge, 56 Buxton Road, Duke of Conaught, 56 Derby Street, Eagle and Child, 33 Newgate, Farmer's Arms, 120 High Street, Feathers Inn, 213 Crompton Road, Friendship Inn, 27 Bond Street, Fruiterers Arms, 27 Buxton Road, Gardeners Arms, 2 Parsonage Street, George and Dragon, 22 Crompton Road, Globe Inn, Hibel Road, Golden Eagle, 5 Mill Street, Grove Inn, 122 Chestergate, Hanging Gate, 71 Hurdsfield Road, Hen and Chicken, 30 Derby Street, Hop Pole, 33 Byrom Street, Horse and Jockey, 52 Mill Lane, Joiner's Arms, 92 Paradise Street, King Edward, 7 King Edward Street, King's Arms, 21 Derby Street, Mechanic's Arms, Waterside, Morning Gun, 15 Mill Lane, New Bridge Inn, Poole Street, Old Red Lion, 61 Sunderland Street, Old Silk Mill, Sunderland Street, Old King's Head, Commercial Road, Old King's Head, Bradley Smithy, Old Plough Inn, 26 Chester Road, Old Turks Head, 25 Waterside, Old Wheat Sheaf, Market Place, Queens Arms, Ryles Street, Red Lion, 160 Hurdsfield, Reform Club, 17 Elizabeth Street, Ring of Bells, 42 King Edward Street, Rising Sun, 27 Jordongate, Roebuck, Union Gateway, Roe Street Tavern, 46 Roe Street, Royal Oak, 87 Mill Street, Shakespeare Inn, 3 Samuel Street, Sir Robert Peel, 65 Bank Street, Sir Robert Peel, Higginbotham Street, Stanley Arms, 11 Stanley Street, Unicorn Hotel, Market Place, Weavers Arms, Bank Street, Wheatsheaf, 10 Stanley Street, Wheatsheaf, 16 Waterloo Street, White Bear, 1 King Edward Street, Wright's Vaults, 23 Mill Street, Ye Old Cheshire Cheese, St. George's Street, Ye Old Derby Arms, 50 Derby Street, Ye Old Wheatsheaf, Mill Green. It may be that one or more of these pubs changed their names between 1910 and my early memories of pubs about 1950.

I now wish to give you some interesting information taken from a survey done in April 1974 by David Hall, Chairman of the South Manchester Branch of CAMRA, The

Campaign for Real Ale. It is called *A Guide to Real Ale Pubs of Macclesfield*. The report lists 61 pubs still serving real ale. Of these there are 17 Robinson's, 13 Allied Ind Coope, 10 Greenall Whitley's, 8 Boddington's, 6 Marston's, 3 Wilson's, and Bass Charrington's, Burton Wood, Higson, and Allied Ansell, one each. In his detailed report it would appear that in his opinion the two best were The Evening Star and The Fool's Nook.

Enough about alcohol, I would now like to turn to non-alcoholic beverages. As a teenager I never had any desire to drink alcohol, unlike teenagers of today some of whom make every effort to drink before they are eighteen. Even when I reached the age when drinking was permitted I never really had the urge to so my visits to pubs were very infrequent. The clamour for alcohol today may have something to do with the loss of the milk bars which were such a feature of the Town when I was growing up. These places, where you could listen to a juke box banging out the latest hit music, were very popular even though they served mainly Vimto hot or cold and warm drinks like Horlicks and Ovaltine made with an early type of expresso machine. You could get snacks like piklets and crumpets, hot and buttered, so in bad weather you never needed to move out and when it was fine the youth of the Town would travel from one milk bar to the next just to see who was there. One thing I know, I never saw any fights although the various gangs would pass in the street and often make challenging remarks. The town had several milk bars and although all the teenagers, boy or girl, had a sort of allegiance to just one, most would in the course of a year visit them all.

I think the oldest one would be the Spa in Mill Street between Roe Street and Exchange Street. I think it was called the Spa. I'm sure it existed during the Second World War as I recall my mother working there for a short period before she went onto the buses as a conductor - or should that be a conductress? It was rather up market and I may be wrong but I do not recall it having a juke box.

Going just around the corner into Queen Victoria Street was the second of our milk bars; was it called the Cavendish? Maybe I am mixed up but I believe it spawned a car club of the same name which thrived for years.

One of my favourites, at the foot of Mill Street on Old Park Lane, I think was called the Rainbow. There is a Rainbow today on Old Mill Lane but that is more of a breakfast haunt for HGV drivers. Anyway the Rainbow used to attract a lot of bikers - cyclists not motorbikes. They came from far and wide on Sunday mornings to this little oasis. One of its visitors was Bob Greaves of Granada TV News who lived in the Sale area.

My local, as you might say, was the one on Mill Lane opposite the Park Green Cenotaph. I think this one was called the Poplar Cafe, and it is now a Tandoori restaurant. We would sit for hours listening to the latest top twenty hits as defined by the NME (New Musical Express) and plugged by Radio Luxembourg on 208 metres or Radio Caroline, broadcasting illegally from somewhere off the coast of England in a boat. The BBC tried in vain to stop their illegal broadcasts. In the end they beat them by playing the same music and calling the station Radio One!

There was a café next to the bus station on Sunderland Street which at one stage was on the other side of the street - in what was originally the local bus company's restaurant and crew room. It was used mostly by those who were waiting for the buses. The teenagers would move on from there to the Bridge Café next to both the railway bridge over the road and the bridge over the River Bollin. I expect its postal address was Gas Road, now a cul-de-sac. It was either the same building or next door to a shop owned by Archie Brough who sold both bicycles and fishing tackle. You will know it, it stood between Johnny Platts car

Rainbow Cafe, Old Mill Lane.

showrooms and the stone masons.

Arrowsmiths café stood on Watersgreen at the foot of the 108 steps and between the two pubs. I have had occasion to go there but it was more like a tearoom for old ladies, with table cloths and small vases of flowers.

At the Victoria Milk Bar in Chestergate near to where the inner relief road cut Chestergate in half, in addition to the usual fare, you could buy at least three flavours of ice cream made on the premises. This was the home of Granelli's Cream Ices, known throughout the town as the best, long before Walls and Lyons cornered the market. It was the new road that caused them to move their operations to Barker's old builder's yard in Newton Street from where they still send out their ice cream vans.

The last of the milk bars I recall I think was the last to open and may well have been the first to close. I cannot remember its name but it was on the ground floor of an old factory on Chestergate opposite the Drome car park at the end of Catherine Street. I always felt that it was a cold and uninviting place, whitewashed walls and no atmosphere. It was more like a works canteen. It was yet another of our buildings to be demolished.

A completely different kind of watering hole ought to receive a mention here. Our beloved baths in Davenport Street, now a house and a car park. Many of us learnt to swim in that building, which had two baths, one for the boys and one for the girls, although I think mixed bathing did occur on occasions. I, like many others, would have been walked from my school, in my case Athey Street, across the Town for a swimming lesson. There were no buses then. It's a wonder the kids of today have not lost the use of their legs!

When the Council took the decision that we should have new swimming baths most of us were delighted until we found out it was to be sited nearer to the centre of Prestbury than the centre of Macclesfield. I, like many others, thought the best site would have been Hibel Road goods yard, now Tesco's car park. There it would have been central for most of us. Now only those with a car seems to be able to use the facilities. It was one of those decisions made by the Council many of whose members come from places like Alderley, Wilmslow, Prestbury and Poynton. The town of Macclesfield is dominated by out of town councillors. It is another bad decision. One only has to see the chaos of the road system outside the leisure centre to see that.

But let us not dwell on my opinion of Macclesfield's elected representatives and move quickly onto another subject of watering holes, and the loss of toilet facilities in the town over the past forty years. I wonder if it was that the Council thought that in this modern age we no longer needed to go to the toilet. I appreciate that over the same period most houses have changed from a privy at the end of the garden and a chamber pot under the bed to the new style en-suite facilities offered with all new houses. The new laws that all premises serving food must supply toilets may be a factor but we still need to go and I suspect the loss of all these facilities, until recently provided by the Town, is down to vandalism, improper use, and shortage of money.

The following sites have vanished: the gents' urinals in Samuel Street and Gladstone Square have been bricked up. The main facility next to the old police station at the side of the Town Hall has its iron gates firmly locked. The large toilet block on Westminster Street has been demolished, a very useful one which stood alongside a bus stop and must have been a welcome site for those having a long wait for a bus. They demolished the one at Broken Cross and the one at the bus station also went without any warning. There were two connected with the cattle market on Waters Green, one at the bottom of Brunswick Hill and one almost under the railway bridge next to Central Station, both long since gone. The other beautiful red brick facility on Waters Green has been replaced by a Dr Who 'Tardis' type unisex box that looks as though it ought to play music. Maybe it does; I have never used it; I would be too worried I could not get out once the door closed.

There was an old pumping station on Chester Road at the end of Field Bank Road, which after use for a short period as a branch library, from 1950 was converted to a toilet, but it did not last very long. We had one in London Road opposite the Catholic Church but this was demolished as was that in the Victoria Park on the corner of York Street. Even the toilets on Park Green are threatened and the only new facilities provided by the Town are on Churchill Way but only open until eight o'clock. Not much use if you have just been turned out of a pub at closing time. Spending a penny in Macclesfield is becoming more difficult. At least, it may have the effect of making more use of our beloved pubs and stop the rapid decline in their numbers!

I hope that it is not all gloom and doom as the architects try to replace all our lovely local stone and Macclesfield brick, or should I say Cheshire, with glass and steel. I do feel we may have passed the worst and that old style building is on the way back. Soon wooden window frame sales may once again outstrip those of plastic .

Public Toilets, Park Green.

108 Steps.

CHAPTER EIGHT
TOWN CENTRE CHANGES

Do you remember the days when all policeman wore tall helmets there was always one to be found standing on traffic duty at the end of Chestergate, directing traffic in front of the Town Hall, resplendent in his uniform with the long white sleeves over his arms? He could be relied upon to leave his post to come and talk to you if you had any sort of query. When Macclesfield boasted a market second to none and it was situated centrally in the Market Place and Waters Green? When tall prams with babies in them stood in rows outside Woolworths whilst the mothers did their shopping without the fear of abduction? When the whole town closed for two weeks at the end of June for the Barnaby holidays and all the mills fell silent as the queues formed outside the railway station for such destinations as Blackpool and Rhyl? When Macclesfield had three local papers The Times, The Courier, and The Advertiser and they all were full of local news which the population was anxious to read? Now it's just The Express, still referred to by older inhabitants as The Times.

Those days have gone for good. Let us look at some of the changes since fifty years ago and the days before flat-pack furniture and B & Q, when the Town had two flourishing sale rooms. Every Wednesday two auctioneers would sell off large quantities of secondhand furniture and bric a brac. One in Great King Street was George Brian's estate agents. George would do the selling assisted by his son. The other in a wooden shed to the rear of Brocklehurst estate agents in King Edward Street was run by Mike Pickwell, an auctioneer who did not require a microphone. He was ably assisted by his porter Derek Ford who was a very knowledgeable gentleman when it came to antiques. He is a regular writer on the subject of old Macclesfield. Their amusing banter was loved by all - it always reminded me of Laurel and Hardy.

Which of you is old enough to remember Blackburn's sweet shop in Chestergate at the corner of Bridge Street? It is now selling motor mowers and chain saws and is run by Geoff Norbury an ex-employee of Parkside Farm. The Blackburns had two children Betty, the eldest was over six foot tall and well known as a national swimmer. Her brother Johnny was 'vertically challenged' but amongst his achievements he was for years the lead drummer in St. John's scout band.

Macclesfield's first Chinese restaurant was in the Market Place and called Min Yin, or was it Ming Ying. A second appeared later in Stanley Street. I had meals in both of them despite the silly rumours which went about that they used tins of Kit-e-Kat and even fed the public with dog meat. The rumours may well have been put about by those who did not relish the competition from foreign food outlets. Today we accept outlets serving foreign food. Even Macdonalds is foreign and some of their food is not to my liking, but it is now the done thing to eat out and try other dishes from other cultures.

The fire station was in Cumberland Street before the street was cut in two by the new road. It occupied the end of the cul-de-sac now used by Wright and Morton's veterinary clinic. I never understood why it moved to Chester Road when at the time the biggest fire hazard was Lower Heys Mills and Parkside Hospital which then could only be accessed from Victoria Road.

I suspect most will remember the new market stalls, known affectionately as "Nuns Hats" due to their appearance. They stood where the new town hall extension is now and they were designed by a young planning officer in the Council's employ. The design was brilliant but there was a strong opposition to them from conservationists at the time.

The rear of Brocklehurst Saleroom, some of which was demolished in 1984.

Nuns' Hats, now sheep shelters and shown on the Ordnance Survey maps.

Despite all the opposition from the public the council gave itself permission to erect the 'hats'in the middle of a conservation area, something which most certainly would have been refused if you or I had made the planning application.

Ironically when they were dismantled to make way for the new town hall extension, and the market was banished to the other side of the Town's dividing road, the unwanted stalls came into my possession. This caused the Council considerable embarrassment and they tried desperately to stop me using or even storing them. They went to considerable lengths costing the ratepayers of the Town a vast amount of money trying to impose their will. After a lengthy appeal the department of the environment agreed with me that my use of the old stalls was not contrary to planning law and to this day the old stalls are still used as sheep shelters. A case of good use and recycling to avoid these fibre glass structures ending up in a land fill site!

The Town centre has changed considerably since the loss of Stanley Street and the building of the Grosvenor Centre. The loss of Derby Street gave us Tesco's supermarket and car park. These changes may well have been for the better, we will never know, but I do not think much consideration was given to any alternative. The Council was at that stage hell bent on changes to the Town and overruled any opposition.

Around the time these changes were taking place the Town had a new police chief, one Inspector McBride. He was credited with the introduction of the Town's one way traffic system, which allowed traffic to go down Mill Street and not up at the junction with the market place, followed by a one way system for Chestergate. The idea was to solve traffic congestion but despite my efforts to point out the problems the scheme went ahead resulting in a traffic flow rotating in the wrong direction. This was the source of most of our traffic problems of today.

Let us now look at some of the fine buildings and shops we have lost, starting with our Town Hall and the surrounding area of the Market Place. The Town Hall was built in 1823-24 by the architect Francis Goodwin and in 1869-71 a wider front was added under supervision of a local architect James Stevens. The building incorporated a police station, a butter market, and public conveniences, all now closed. In those days all the roads would have been cobbled, most now dug up and sold to adorn private drive ways, or covered in tarmac.

With the removal of the market from in front of the Town Hall and the pedestriani-sation of both Chestergate and Mill Street, the Council had a good opportunity to replan the area in front of St. Michael's Church. After spending thousands of pounds on the project we have finished up with an Italian style piazza which does not appear to have won much support from the Populus. The area is now underused and decorated with someone's idea of modern wrought iron seats which are neither pretty or comfortable. The sooner they go the better. I hope, along with many Maxonians, as expressed in a poll conducted by the local paper, that we will soon have our market back where it belongs. This move has long been resisted by Council officers who give various reasons why it is not possible or practical. It is high time they considered who they work for. They are our employees and they would do well to remember that. It is our town and if we want a market in front of the Town Hall who is to say we cannot have it there?

Whilst the new surface in front of the Town Hall is pleasant - but not cobblestones which would have worn better - it does attract vast amounts of chewing gum dropped by the public. I always thought that spitting and chewing gum were two of the most undesirable habits of mankind, only marginally better than dog excrement on pavements.

Town Hall, built 1823-24.

Churchside.

Churchside.

Old police station and
public conveniences.

Goose Lane, now called Brunswick Hill.

Having got that grouse out of my system let's look at the area. The narrow street system around the church has changed very little. Churchside is still dominated by solicitors' offices and Church Wall Gate, now apparently renamed Church Street, is the home for a number of estate agents. The cottages to the side of the Town Hall, in the ownership of the Council, and up till recently used as offices, are now all boarded up and look ripe for demolition.

There was of course once a castle which stood roughly on the site now occupied by Mothercare, previously Marks and Spencers. Parts of the old wall can still be seen half way down Back Wall Gate and it is said that there are underground passages between the church and the castle. There still remains the public house called the Castle half way down the slope and evidence has been found of a graveyard on the top side of Queen Victoria Street.

Some of Macclesfield's more attractive features can still be seen to the rear of the Town Hall on Hawthorn Street, saved from the planners because of the steepness of the slope down to Waters Green. The area is known as Sparrow Park and has three sets of steps going down to the old cattle market area of the Town. The 108 Steps are well known but Step Hill in the centre and Brunswick Hill to the north are not so well known. With the increase in car use these steps do not see too many pedestrians, at least not the number there would have been one hundred years ago.

Great efforts have been made to improve and maintain this historical part of the town but they have been thwarted by the drunks, junkies and graffiti artists. I expect the drunks might have been there years ago but the litter problem was not so great before fast foods and Macdonalds polystyrene cartons.

Now cast your mind back to a time when Walter Isaac was the town clerk; one shop you would recognise was that of Leslie Black which stood between Barclays Bank and Brunswick Street. The shop was distinctive because of its large clock hanging over the front in the days before we all got fitted up with digital watches. Black's sold gents' clothing and riding equipment, that is horse riding. Opposite them was Goodwin's who sold office stationery and did some printing. Next to them was Hodgson's who sold radios and later television. Between there and the Bulls Head was the well known grocery store of Seymour Mead.

Market Place. Hodgsons and Goodwins.

Boot's Chemist, taken down in 1979.

On the corner of Chestergate was Boots the Chemist now long gone to make way for the employment exchange or whatever fancy name it was given when it moved from South Park Road. Further along and just below the Angel Hotel was W.H.Smiths which now stands lower down Mill Street, They advertised as booksellers and librarians. Next to them was a building which seems to have survived unscathed, that of Chester Twemlows, tobacconist. This black and white building shows a date of 1397. I used to call there in the days when I was a smoker, long before it was discovered to be detrimental to health. It was one of the few shops that sold Passing Cloud ciggies, an up market brand which was oval in shape and must have made me feel a little superior to other smokers of my generation.

Next to them was Redman's who advertised "Good Bacon and Dried Fruit". On the opposite corner of Stanley Street, now the Grosvenor Centre, was Hadfields and across the road from them was Leech and Son, Dispensing Chemist.

As we proceeded down Mill Street we passed McFisheries where we could always smell the unmistakable odour of fresh fish and on the other side of the street was Burtons with its upstairs rooms catering for both snooker and dancing. Burtons was best known as the fifty shilling tailor (or, as it would be now, the two pound fifty pence tailor), the price for a new made-to-measure suit then. I do believe that the shop gave rise to the saying "gone for a Burton", a reference perhaps to the fact that all servicemen when demobbed were given money to buy a civilian suit to replace the uniform in which they had served their Country.

I think all the top part of Mill Street, down to Queen Victoria Street, has, with one exception, been rebuilt on a building line set back from the original, making the street wider than it would have been one hundred years ago. The one exception I believe is that of Roses Shoe Shop, now under a different name and next to Mothercare.

Other shops in Mill Street you may remember are Pegram and Mason's, grocers; Ripolin, paints and wallpaper; Pages, ladies dresses for those that could afford them; a gent's outfitters called Hepworth's; and more recently Lekerman's a cut price store.

Newday's furniture store was on the site of the old Albert Inn referred to in chapter seven, and was demolished along with the rest of Derby Street to make room for the new Marks and Spencers. Lower down was the old Norweb store where you could pay your electric bill before they were taken over by United Utilities and bills paid by direct debit.

Mill Street had at least two jewellers. One was on the corner of Queen Victoria Street where I regularly went for my watch repairs. I recall a very pleasant gentleman behind the counter, a Scotsman I suspect. Was the shop a branch of H. Samuels? - no that was somewhere else. The other was on the corner of Pickford Street, later demolished after a fire made the building unsafe. That was Breeze's, a gentleman who I think served on the Town Council for some time in the 1950s. Somewhere in Mill Street, I think near to Breeze's, was a jewellers called Morleys and I am also just reminded of Jones in Chestergate. They all made a good living selling watches and rings.

On the opposite side of Mill Street, near the corner of Roe Street, was Brammer's butchers recognised easily by the shop front glazed with light brown tiles. Another very interesting shop was that of Charles Day's who sold almost everything in the hardware line. I can see his galvanised buckets hanging outside over the footpath and a row of dustbins, not plastic, obstructing the pavement. It could not happen now - if someone fell over them they would immediately think about suing for damages. The fact is we are following the United States in blaming everyone else for our misfortunes, we no longer take responsibility for our own actions. Our first thought now, as we see daily on our television

Newday's furnishings on the corner of Derby Street.

Mayor's Sunday parade outside the Parish Church. Drum Major, the author, Stanley Albinson, the Parade Marshall. The front row of St. John's drum and bugle band are Roy Barton, Johnny Blackburn and Jim Rose.

Paige's dress shop 1977
opposite Woolworths.

Marks and Spencer
store, now
Mothercare.

Rose and Hepworths,
Mill Street, 1973.

Mill Street 1979.
Norweb and Ripolin.

screens, is "I am consulting my solicitor with a view to taking legal action". Yes it's always someone else's fault!

Back to the subject. Mill Street had the Rope Shop. It's difficult to see how one could make a living by selling rope, although they did in fact sell other things, and this was before polyester and nylon fibres. Around the corner in Queen Victoria Street was Jones' music shop where in addition to sheet music and guitars you could arrange for your piano to be tuned or buy the latest hit on a 78 r.p.m. record. No CDs then; in fact we were only just getting used to non-wind up gramophones and extended play seven inch plastic records.

Somewhere along Mill Street we had Burdine's grocers and Wilson's Army and Navy Stores, which still exists today in Chestergate. Finally in Mill Street we had a chemist shop between Duke Street and the Majestic Cinema which displayed a similar clock over its doorway as that of Leslie Black's.

If we now take a look along Chestergate we had the U.C.P., which in addition to selling tripe and cow heel was known mainly for the rich aroma of fresh ground coffee which wafted along the street. This was also a very popular place for office workers to take their lunch breaks. Almost opposite was Holland and Barwoods, who sold soft furnishings and other goods to make our homes comfortable, and a few doors away the Singer sewing machine shop where a relative of my mother used to work. A lot of you will have had a Singer in your home to run up new clothes and repair the old ones. That was in the days of 'make do and mend' when most of us could not afford new. Whilst we were not all wearing clogs and living on jam butties, times were not so easy and we relied on the female side of our families to keep the home together, whilst the men went out to work. Today we live in a throwaway society which means we send more things to land fill sites than ever before. Strangely enough, though, I think there was more work in the Town then for women than there was for men.

One place you will remember was the Advertiser office, where one could call and see Alan Oliver, the editor, at any time. He was over six foot in height and was well known for his activities with the Chamber of Trade. I will always remember him as the secretary of the Agricultural Society which held shows each year in the South Park until financial problems hit the Society of which I was a founder member.

Almost opposite the Advertiser was a shop called Ray Wood's who sold items which interested me so much I would spend time just looking in their window - Meccano, Hornby trains, Dinky toys and aircraft model kits; it fascinated me. Plastic was not around in those days but its forerunner was being used, Bakelite. It came into use for domestic goods as well as toys. The first plastics I think came with the Frido Football, made locally at Lower Heyes factories. I think it was V. and E. Friedlands who started it.

Quite near to Woods was A. Whiting's, a sports shop whose displays included tennis racquets, cricket bats and for the very rich even skis. I remember one or two other places of interest; Ashton's Leather Goods in Derby Street and Atlas Printing Works. They did the posters for the local football club when they were in the Cheshire League. Most events were advertised by their posters at that time although there were other printers in the Town.

Jordongate had Jackson's who supplied goods to the office trade, as did Till's of Lord Street who moved to the Hovis factory before ceasing trading; the supply of paper clips and the like could not sustain their business.

One business which has done much for the Town is The Cheshire Building Society who in addition to building a new office in Castle Street made a wonderful job of restoring the old post office building on the corner of Castle Street and the new Churchill Way. Other

Chestergate, 1970. Universal Carpets next to the Advertiser.

Ashton Shop, Derby Street. Note the all stone structure.

Atlas Printing Works Derby Street.

Jackson's on Jordongate.

Churchill Way 1980.

Old Cheshire Building Society offices next to Woolworth's rear entrance.

Old Post Office sorting office, now Cheshire Building Society.

Pickford Street 1973.

areas of the Town centre have been levelled for development, not all of it as good as the Cheshire Building Society offices.　Take for instance the lower end of Pickford Street cleared for a Co-op building which changed hands and is now itself to be demolished to make way for a bus station and a cinema, if we are lucky.　I do not think there was anything wrong with the old bus station except that the town moved away from it with the effective closure of Sunderland Street to traffic when they opened the bypass.

Lastly I would like to give a mention to the famous Prospect Buildings.　They may have had a somewhat murky past and to have lived there may not have been one the best starts in life, but it was a community.　It has been replaced by a superstore, now T.J. Hughes, a fine company but not a very nice building, and its delivery entrance over the years has caused more heartaches for the people of Roe Street than the residents of Prospect Buildings ever did.

Prospect Buildings.

The old Co-op shop in Commercial Road.

Copper Street.

CHAPTER NINE
THE WHOLESALE DESTRUCTION OF COMMUNITIES

Over the last fifty years, on the pretext of removing 'slums' and rehousing people, the Town has had huge sections of its housing reduced to rubble and whole communities moved, often against their will, to new estates on the edge of Town.

The Moss estate was built before the last War. Both the Hurdsfield and Weston Estates were built on green field sites after the War providing cheap and affordable houses most of which were Council housing. The Upton Priory Estate was the last one to be built, the finance for it predominantly from Salford City Council as it was to house their overspill.

When the Moss was built it was planned and built to a very high standard considering the building technology of that period. The Hurdsfield estate started with just the Crescent on Hurdsfield Road well before Queen's Avenue cut through the centre of it. A new road now called Hulley Road was cut at a point which had been a dirt cul-de-sac by the name of Cow Lane with just a few cottages on one side. Beyond the few cottages was a narrow track between two high privet hedges which concealed allotment gardens. Parts of the original track can still be seen on the left of Hulley Road, the footpath alongside a few trees. This track went on past a stream towards the Red Barn as it was known, an isolated farm building in the middle of green fields which was the centre of many unlikely stories!

In the mid-1940s a start was made on the Weston Estate, named after the Town's MP, Garfield Weston, who achieved some fame as the inventor of Westons Wagon Wheels a chocolate biscuit still made today. The name did not, as many people seem to think, come from the geographical position of the estate to the Town. I was very small at the time but I do recall them starting the new road off Ivy Lane which later was to be called Earlsway.

The new estate at Upton swamped the Town's only public bridleway which ran from Prestbury Road to Priory Lane. It is still there but now strewn with glass and badly neglected. Since the finance for this estate came from Salford City Council most of the new tenants were from the City and many of them could not stand the clean air and open fields. Their loss of close neighbours caused many of them to return to Salford. The houses themselves were built to a very poor standard and despite advice at the time had flat roofs to keep the cost down. This was not a saving as after only a few years it was necessary to put pitched roofs on all of them at great expense to the ratepayers of the Town.

Devastation was achieved in a very curious way. The Council would designate an area for redevelopment and this would blight all the properties so much so that tenants would not spend money on their homes and landlords were even more reluctant to do any repairs. This had the effect of running down an area to such an extent that it became an eyesore and gave the Council an excuse to schedule for demolition. Even if an appeal was heard it was almost inevitable that, due to the run-down state of the properties, the inspector would side with the Council. They would then be in a position to acquire the properties under a compulsory purchase order. Tenants would be paid market value, dependant on the state of the property which was often not enough to allow the owner occupier enough money to rehouse by buying their own so they would become a Council tenant. The landlord was even worse off as he would only get the value of the site, which in many cases was as little as one hundred and fifty pounds.

Quite often families would be moved out on the grounds that the houses were not habitable and then they would be boarded up. Then vandals and squatters between them would take all the lead, the light fittings and sometimes even set fire to the properties.

Windmill Street, corner of Copper Street.

Dereliction gave the Council an excuse to evict and acquire the rest of the houses at the lowest possible price.

Often developers would buy up the properties and encourage this degradation of the area allowing weeds to grow and rats to flourish. This was the way the game was played.

This happened all over the Town until one day a young up and coming architect by the name of Rod Hackney found his own home on Black Road threatened with similar destruction. He fought the local council and won the argument and the battle. He then set about the renovation of all the properties in the row with the full support of the other residents. His success was rewarded with a plaque on the side of his home and an official opening by his friend the Prince of Wales.

This one event had an effect on the Council's policy and caused a major change of direction. This change was reflected in the High Street area which became a conservation area and many of the houses were saved from the bulldozer. It is a great regret that this change of attitude did not come about in time to save the community around Victoria Park. We all know now how wrong the planning officers were when they built the 'Vicky Park Flats'. The councillors boasted at the time of their great achievement but I think they all now admit it was a colossal failure. They are now to be demolished and hopefully rebuilt in a similar style to the original. I hope that this time they will listen to the people who will have to live there. These so called experts find dictating a way of life to others a 'turn on'. They create homes which they themselves would not live in. Perhaps the planners and architects will get together with the people and build it right this time. The problem is that those who plan and build will take their profit and run to the country - or even another, warmer country - and never look back to see what their profit taking has created.

The Vicky flats were a bad example but it was not just an isolated mistake. We often hear on the television when a crime is perpetrated that an area is a "closely knit community"; well there are only a few of them left in Macclesfield. There was a day when all neighbours left their doors unlocked; if anything was stolen it was usually known who would have done it. Everyone knew everyone else and a stranger in the neighbourhood would soon be recognised. There was very little need for the police. Now if you are burgled the police rarely bother to investigate the crime. It seems to me that their attitude

Cundiff's Shop, Windmill Street.

now is, there is no point in investigating as the crime will not be solved and anyway it probably was your own fault for not having security locks on all doors and windows. Today it turns out that it is your own fault and not that of the offender.

The days are long gone when you knew your next door neighbour. Most people today do not even know the people next door. They just sit at home watching the box in the corner and only going out to the pub or to shop or to work (and not even this in all cases).

Much of this condition has been caused by councils trying to rationalise areas under their control. They did not seem to understand the damage they were doing - or they didn't care. Many of us still remember the Victoria Park area before the flats. The shops, the pubs and the community were destroyed along with the houses and the churches. When Rod Hackney showed the Council the way, the blight was curtailed to a degree but it did not save the area around Copper street. We lost a butchers, a newsagents and Mrs Cundiff's shop on the corner of Black Road and Windmill Street. I do not think she wanted to go, but go she did and her only reward was to have a street named after her!

The change of attitude has benefited the High Street area. Many of the houses were upgraded under a scheme which made it a conservation area. Unfortunately this was done at the expense of the road layout which deliberately funnelled all the traffic onto Mill Lane so as to massage the traffic census figures to justify the building of the Silk Road.

We did however lose the parts between Byrom Street and White Street along with the Hop Pole and the School and the church. When they flattened this area they somehow forgot Higginbotham Green - was it just an oversight.

Another area blitzed and replaced with a car park for the Mercedes Garage was the area of Statham Street, Union Street and Elizabeth Street, an area commonly known as The Dams. A well known feature of the Town, The Dams Steps are still there, but no one ever sees them because they closed the road which accessed the top of the steps and built over it. It is now part of Sutton Engineering. They did however recognise the steps by placing a monument to the industrial age; a circular saw bench. A nice thought but of little purpose in this isolated position. Along with all the houses went the church of St. John and up came all the graves - not even the dead were left in peace. One place you may remember on Statham Street was Arthur Smith's shop where I often called to buy a 16's hook and a tin

Cross Street, Coronation Street.

Cross Street, Byrom Street, March 1980.

Higginbotham Green, still standing.

Byrom Street, March 1980.

Rear of Statham Street.

Statham Street - ripe for clearance.

Above: Bower's Chemist, corner of
Windmill Street and Mill Lane.

Right: Dean Street, Windmill Square 1970

Dams Steps.

of maggots for my fishing expedition to the South Park. You could buy them in white, pink, and a yellow although I am not convinced that fish can see colour!

When we lost Statham Street, we did not just lose a church but we lost Globe and Simpsons and we isolated the garages of Thornley the removal people. The yard was later taken on by Ray Naden the coach operator who also owned the George Hotel for a time. I do not know who owns it now but it is still filled with old vehicles and various scrap and is an ideal site for some builder to put a few houses on - I wonder how they missed this prime site. Maybe it's in the Town's new structure plan for early clearance.

Another little hamlet was lost when they cleared Windmill Square and the surrounding roads to make way for another yard for lorries and small industry. I once courted a girl who lived at the top of Dean Street but I can't recall her name. That was in the days when gas lamps outnumbered the new sodium discharge lighting!

Part of Mill Lane had to go when they terminated the new Silk Road in the wrong place. It now spills out all its traffic onto a narrow and most unsuitable road south, already swamped by the traffic forced off High Street by the street closure policy, a policy introduced I believe because when the Town's football team played at home much of the traffic avoided the hold up at Park Green by cutting through the side streets to get to Park Lane. I can still remember back far enough to when London Road was blocked with pedestrian traffic after a match. The talk now is of re-siting the football ground.

Do you remember Les Crohn's flower shop on the Sutton-Macclesfield boundary and Bowers Chemist on the corner of Windmill Street. We also lost shops in between such as Mrs Bell's butchers and Arther Hayes' furnishings. I suspect there are still many homes with a settee provided by Hayes.

Park Green lost a nice row of shops when they cleared the area around Parsonage Street. The brewery went, along with a good snooker hall which I frequented occasionally on unauthorised school holidays. Much of it was sacrificed in favour of the motor car and its storage for those who do not like walking. Baroness Boutique, Mabel's hairdressers, The Pet Shop, and a newsagents, all went in a flash. Now the other side of Parkgreen is under a cloud, a few of its old buildings have already been replaced and the rest are under threat.

The biggest calamity of modern times is the total destruction of Parkside Hospital where I worked as a wages clerk for three and a half years. With a farm, a laundry, a printers shop, it was a total community serving over one thousand patients and a similar number of employees, many living in the grounds. To see it today is heartbreaking, an area of utter destruction just so someone can make a lot of money. There is little evidence that we need all these new houses, but we shall have them anyway. We are tempted by offers of 100% mortgages and flashy front doors but they will not replace the community they destroy. I do not know if putting all those ill patients out into the community is right or wrong; the government says it saves money - and the sale of the land for building certainly makes money, at least for a few - but not for the exiled patients.

Many agree that the area could have been better used for parkland and old peoples' sheltered homes, but that idea is not profitable. Changes were needed maybe, but I for one believe the changes only benefit a few speculators who will take the money and go to live in the country, or Prestbury, or abroad. It is a fact that money, or more correctly the love of money, is the root of all evil.

Park Green, Parsonage Street.

Parkside Hospital under demolition 1999.

Chestergate 1978, demolished for Churchill Way.

CHAPTER TEN
ROADS OLD AND NEW

In a period before I was born, a time most of you will not remember either, the town planners of the day must have had great foresight and vision. They anticipated the huge growth in traffic along with the growth of the town to such a degree . The evidence is still there to see. When they built the Moss Estate they built Western Avenue as a bypass wide enough for four lanes of traffic. Although it was at that time to the south of the town, it was to be the Western Bypass. A part of Western Avenue can still be seen at the top of Ryles Park Road and a line passing across Congleton Road and up Thornton Avenue was for years a line protected from the builders. The road was to have continued across Gawsworth Road, and across Chelford Road between Henbury Church and Broken Cross, to come out onto the Manchester Road near to Beech Hall School. This road if it had been built would have removed all the north south traffic from the town.

Unfortunately it was scuppered, probably by councillors who lived in Knowsley and Ryles Park Road. It appears that they influenced the decision to build old persons' bungalows on the centre of Western Avenue. It is now disguised by the re-naming of one side as Robin Hood Avenue. This action put an end once and for all to the idea of a Western bypass. In its place a new line was proposed and protected. This was to start on Moss Lane near to the Isolation Hospital and go diagonally across the traffic lights at the top of Park Lane and down past All Hallows School to emerge onto Chester Road at Field Bank Road. This was before the school was built. The idea was to continue across the cricket ground to join up with Manchester Road.

This idea was sunk by those who either played cricket for the town or friends of the cricket club who did not like the idea of losing their ground. There is still a possibility of a part of the road being built from the Lyme Green Business Park or as it would be better called The Moss Estate Retail Park. A line from London Road through the retail park and onto the Congleton Road has been agreed but what cannot be agreed is who will pay for a bridge over the railway.

Over the years our representatives on the Council change and different interests prevail. These changes result in plans and proposals by one set of people being changed by the next lot. When the crunch finally came and the traffic problem was put into the hands of the Northern Road Construction unit on behalf of the Ministry of Transport, they saw only a disused railway line. This line, which was cut by Dr Beeching as not required or not viable, was an ideal and cheap route. It did not matter if the route was suitable so long as it was cheap. As a result we may have the only town in the country whose bypass runs through the town and not round it.

The only thing they had to decide was where it should start and finish. The sensible idea would have been to start at Dunbah Lane in the north and finish at Star Lane in the south. This was not accepted for two reasons. One, there was not enough money for the whole length so it would be terminated short of its sensible southern end. The other, that those in Prestbury did not relish the idea of it finishing at Dunbah Lane as it might encourage traffic to cut through the village, so pressure was put on to have it finish further north near Flash Lane.

There was an enquiry but as normal at most of these enquiries, those with the most money usually win. Despite the opposition from the conservationists who wanted to protect the wildlife in Dunbah Hollow the road came first. This extension to the north put an end to any idea of going further south so all the traffic would be left to spill out onto an already overloaded Mill Lane.

Even under construction errors were made, most notably the pillars supporting the road across the River Bollin were out of line and had to be rebuilt. Then the road markings at the roundabout on Hibel Road caused traffic chaos until they realised that they should have shown two lanes and not three on the approaches. The synchronised traffic lights did not function correctly and had to be altered. When it was discovered that to avoid the hill down Buxton Road the heavy lorries were using Brook Street as a short cut onto the new road, they found a solution. You or I might have imposed a weight restriction on Brook Street but not these clever road engineers. They came up with a novel idea. They put a no left turn from Brook Street onto the Silk Road. This had the effect of forcing all the traffic straight across the Silk Road and down to Sunderland Street through the traffic lights on Park Green, along Mill Lane through another set of traffic lights back up onto the Silk Road. Marvellous thinking. It makes one proud to be British, with our wonderfully clever planners.

This was not the limit of their absurdity. The opening of the new by-pass was delayed for several weeks. For what you may well ask. Because a foot bridge was not in place. Why was it not in place? Because it was made in Holland and was not completed on time. I am amazed that with our skills we could not have built a wooden footbridge in England.

Let's leave our by-pass and look at some of the other road building fiascos. Take the turning onto the Industrial Estate off London Road now called Winterton Way. This was put in at council tax payers expense some ten years before it was needed and it even displayed a road sign showing Manchester straight ahead when it was clear that no turning actually existed at that time.

Now let us consider Churchill Way, the new road to run from Hibel Road to Park Lane. The plan was to demolish Corbishley's filling station and cut through the middle of Cumberland Street. Compulsory purchases were made which included the garage. Then someone objected to the line. It was rethought and a new line suggested coming out onto Beech Lane near to where they had just given planning approval for a Methodist Chapel to be built.

Corbishley's garage was reprieved and, under the name of an old school pal, David Bayley started selling petrol again. But the new line brought opposition from the Kings School as it meant they would lose a corner off their cricket field.

Eventually a deal was done with the Kings School which involved the school getting the use of Pearl Street Dyeworks as extra classrooms and the route of the road was put back to the original line. So once again the filling station had to go.

Once the new road was under construction - designed by those who quite clearly had never driven a bus or an articulated lorry, it became obvious that a schoolboy could have done a better job. Its alignment left a lot to be desired. The errors stayed and the traffic had to just get used to them.

As the road cut through the Town centre dividing Chestergate into two halves they had a problem with the junction at Castle Street. They spent time and money lowering the road some eighteen inches for reasons which were never clearly explained.

Probably the silliest part of the design of Churchill Way was the roundabout at its southern end. After a large amount of demolition they found it necessary to close off the end of High Street. No one will ever know who thought up this idea or why it was necessary.

Mill Lane, 1970. The shops cleared for the end of the Silk Road.

Buxton Road 1969, Arthur Watling's motor cycle shop.

Coare Street, 1974, fish and chip shop.

Below: Cumberland Street 1982 - houses demolished for Churchill Way.

Palace Terrace, Hibel Road, 1979.

Hibel Road, 1979, chip shop.

1982. East West Road from Hibel Road.

1982. East West Road from Beech Lane.

Hibel Road demolished for the new East West Road.

Bayleys Garage cleared for the new road.

Let us not criticise everything as one piece of new road I did think was sensible, although at the time there were a lot of local objections. The joining up of Cumberland Street to Chester Road at its junction with Oxford Road seemed to me to be a good idea. It is a shame it was spoilt with the closure of Prestbury road - thought by some to be as a result of Lord Sainsbury paying for some of the work.

In addition to the new roads there have been a few changes to some of our internal roads. For some time the residents of Oxford Road tried in vain to have the through traffic taken from their doorsteps and re-routed down Park Lane with a possible new road being cut along the line of Crompton Road. This had little support due to the high cost of paying compensation to residents of Crompton Road. What actually happened was speed humps and weight restrictions on Ivy Lane, thus increasing traffic on Oxford Road. To show willing they improved the road camber near to the school and put in a pelican crossing. To slow down traffic, which ignored the 30 mph speed limit, they put in a series of islands and altered the colour of the road surface in places. This had no effect on the number of vehicles per hour and did not reduce the tailbacks on Congleton Road and Oxford road one iota.

Being happy with their achievements - that is the highways engineers not the residents of Oxford Road - they went on to introduce more speed humps and road narrowing on Valley Road with a view to causing more delays to through traffic. I suppose traffic jams do slow down the traffic and therefore reduce the accident rate to pedestrians even if they cause road rage in the motorists!

It does seem to me that the lesson is never learnt. My 'O' level in mathematics tells me that if you reduce traffic on one road by whatever means it must increase the traffic on another road. Gone are the days when the locals would find a short cut to avoid the jams along so called 'rat runs' - a name which implies the motorists are vermin.

A similar approach was adopted on Hulley Road. Although it was built as a service road for ICI and Geigy, two of the towns largest employers, once the Silk Road was opened they tried all means to stop the traffic along Hulley Road. Their efforts had the result of HGVs coming down from Rainow to the Hurdsfield Industrial Estate having to go right down the Hurdsfield Road, across Tesco's roundabout, along the Silk Road to approach the estate from the other end of Hulley Road. This only increased the pressure on Hibel Road. Who knows it may have been a contributory factor in the collapse of the sewers and the flooding of Garden Street.

They have recently closed Queen Victoria Street to all vehicles except buses putting more pressure on Sunderland Street and Pickford Street. They have now successfully pedestrianised both Mill Street and Chestergate. Their first attempt at closing Chestergate to traffic as an experiment was abandoned after only a few days.

Even our trunk roads have an effect on all of us. Take for instance the upgrading of the A34 with its by-passes around both Wilmslow and Handforth. It was clear to many of us that it would increase the numbers of commuters choosing a route which passed through the village of Prestbury. Now the residents of that village are taking their own traffic census in an effort to combat the problem. With careful thought and consultation the problem could have been averted.

Finally I must tell of the fiasco of Broken Cross where the pupils from several schools in the area treat the highway as an extension of the footpath. They wander across Chelford Road as if they were invulnerable to the modern motor car. This sadly is not always the case. When they planned the improvement of this busy junction there was a long debate over traffic lights versus roundabout - the latter, being the choice of the planners, won the day. Three fatal accidents have made the planners rethink. We may yet get traffic lights but in the meantime we have temporary, experimental new lanes which if nothing else causes a much greater build up of standing traffic at peak times. This may reduce the casualty rate but, again, does nothing for the road rage of the drivers.

The people who design our roads have a very difficult job to do but I wish sometimes they would just use some commonsense. They tend to follow what others have done like the day they introduced a blue parking disc scheme which they told us had worked in other towns. It did not work here and was soon abandoned after a very expensive experiment.

I would venture a suggestion. All housing which have no arterial roads going through them could be pedestrianised. Treat the roads as footpaths and vice-versa and remove all the kerbs. Allow the pedestrian the main right of way at all times putting the responsibilty squarely on the driver for all accidents. This would have other benefits such as cars not breaking the law by parking on the footpath. Also as cars would park closer to the properties, it would become easier for the dustbin lorry to negotiate the areas. Just think the police fire and ambulance would be able to get to your house in an emergency again! In many streets at the moment this is not the case.

Perhaps this radical change of giving the roads back to the pedestrian is too far sighted for the planners to understand yet. Maybe in twenty years time they will think of it and put it forward as their own idea. In the meantime we are prepared still to accept the sacrifice of many of our children as a by product of car ownership.

Another radical idea might be to ban the parking of all motor vehicles on the highway after dark without lights. The only reason we now permit this parking without lights is because the police did not have time to enforce the old laws so the law was changed. Even today as many as forty percent of cars parked on the road at night do so in contravention of the regulations but the police do nothing to combat this abuse.

It will need some firm action soon if the motor car, already a god, is not to totally rule our lives. The next ten years will decide it. I do long for the days to return when you could play football in the street.

Waterside.

CHAPTER ELEVEN
ODDS & ENDS

When I look around this old town of ours there are still many sites which have evaded the developer and they bring back good memories of the past for me. In this chapter I would like to refresh your memories about a few places and events which have not yet found a place in the book.

Places like the Barracks in Crompton Road, now turned into living accommodation and at one time partly used as a night club. It must at some stage in its life have been used by troops; its structure alone indicates military occupation. One can, when looking at the beautiful stone structure of unique design, imagine the scene with row upon row of uniformed soldiers parading across its open square.

The alms houses in Cumberland Street have survived many of the changes in the Town and still stand as a monument to the builders who worked so skilfully in natural stone. The Town has many other alms house, most of them are situated on the edge of town and not so central as these.

In the days before central heating and plastic window frames most of our homes were heated by coal fires. At the bottom of Hibel Road stood a row of wooden offices of coal merchants who would originally have had horses and carts but in my day mainly had small vans to deliver the one hundred weight bags of nutty slack. There was the Co-op, Welch's, Brierley's, and others whose offices were manned all day to take orders for deliveries and take payment.

Many houses kept coal in bunkers in the yard, perhaps a few did even keep coal in the bath, but most had a cellar. In the front of these houses with a cellar was an iron grid which the coalman lifted up to tip the black gold out of his sacks down the chute. He would pile up the empty bags on one side so the customer could check the delivery before paying.

A mill which I omitted to mention was the Paradise Mill in Old Park Lane. I do not know how it got that name as I am sure it would not have been paradise for those who worked there. They would have had long hours, six days week, and would have to put up with noisy machinery, dusty atmosphere and probably also heat. It would have been a very unhealthy climate and dangerous as well. The mill has been preserved as a working museum and one should go to see it to get a real feel of the past.

Whilst in that area of the Town I think our old library deserves a mention. It was built in 1876 and was a gift to the Town from one David Chadwick, long before the County took over responsibility for libraries. Outside the front of the building was a fountain, the only remains of which now is the circle of stone edgings where it stood. I expect it was made of cast iron and removed as part of the War effort. Some may remember the library when it still had its impressive stone steps up to the main entrance. These were still in situ when John Mills came to the Town to use the library was used as a film set. Many Maxonians were extras in the film. I was a member of the library for only a short time but I did manage to read all the Romany books they had.

Just across the road from the library was another very beautiful building, that latterly of Nat West Bank. Its lovely stonework was blackened over the years by soot from factory chimneys and our coal fires on which many of us cooked our one hot meal of the day. One did not pop out to Macdonalds in those days for a hamburger, or telephone for a pizza.

Only yards from this old bank was a monument to our industrial history. The remnants of the old boiler foundations of Heath's Silk Mills in Charlotte Street were behind

The Barracks, Crompton Road.

Alms House, Cumberland Street.

Grid to cellar. Relic of the coal age.

Below: Paradise Mill, Old Park Lane, 1979.

Macclesfield's old library.

Nat West Bank, Park Green.

Foundations of the boilers at Heath's Silk Mill in Charlotte Street.

The end of the LNER line 1981, after Beeching.

the bus station. The foundations stood alone there for a long time after the factory was removed, a stark reminder of the age of steam when all our factories were run from one or two large engines by a series of belts. In those days many were injured by the machinery as little thought was given to the fitting of safety guards. That would have been considered an unnecessary expense - employees could be easily replaced.

In March 1963 Dr Beeching closed the railway line to Bollington and beyond, and with it went the weighbridge and the little row of coal merchants huts. Soon after we were to lose our gasworks where many a family had queued for a bag of coke - that is coal with the gas removed, not the drink. All the stores connected with the gas industry went to Stockport and we were left with only the gasometer in Garden Street. I was fascinated with the way it rose up during the week and fell on Sunday when all families were at home cooking the lunch. The coal fire was in retreat then and gas use for cooking, before electricity and the microwave, became the norm in most households.

We lost a row of houses in Elizabeth Street when Statham Street went. Some of you will remember the Macclesfield steps in front of the doors to keep out the flood waters which often swamped the area when the Dams Brook ran high, on its way from Broken Cross, via Chester Road, to Waters Green and the Bollin. Some of these cottages were used, I am told, as a Zion Mission.

As a contrast the houses on Richmond Hill never experienced flooding even though they were on the banks of the canal. They overlooked the playing fields known locally as the tip but correctly called St. George's playing fields. It has been used for years by the local dog population as a public convenience and as the site for a large bonfire every year to celebrate the actions of Guy Fawkes. Efforts by the local community over the years to make it into a nice play area for the children have been thwarted by the continual misuse of the site and the vandalism.

Who remembers the old steam laundry in Brough Street West, and the little vans which used to scuttle round the town collecting your laundry? This was in the days before the coin-in-the-slot launderette, which itself has largely now disappeared. Now almost every house has an automatic washing machine. No more using the dolly tub and dolly peg and the little blue bags which miraculously made the clothes white. Did you know that on the roof of that laundry was an air raid siren? I do not know if it was ever used other than for testing since Macclesfield did not suffer directly from the German bombing, only being caught by a few strays which missed Manchester by some distance.

If you never heard the air raid siren you probably remember the factory hooters which went off with precision timing to help the workers get to their benches on time. No one had a digital watch in those days.

There are still a few places where cottages have survived which are worth a visit before they also go. Try Short Street which joins Waters Green to the 108 Steps. All now offices but it's still the shortest street - although I expect Grape Street holds the record for the least number of houses, one.

The shops on Chester Road near Pinfold Street still manage to survive, even if they do not stand in a vertical plane. Maybe they were built like that by a builder who had lost his plumb line. Given a reduction in traffic they may stand a hundred years more, unless of course a speculator spots the sites potential for re-development!

Two other areas which have gone; first Lower Exchange Street off Queen Victoria Street, formerly known as Pudding Bag Lane, I cannot think why. It even had a school there once. Soon it is to become a bus station if the Council's plans for the area materialise.

LNER line viaduct over the River Bollin, demolished 1981.

Elizabeth Street.

Richmond Hill,
demolished 1978.

Air raid siren,
Brough Street West
laundry roof.

Short Street.

Chester Road corner of Pinfold Street.

Lower Exchange Street.

Co-op, Bank Street.

The other area was at the top of Bank Street where all the houses were cleared around the area of Knight's Pool. We lost Lomas's coach station and a number of other smaller businesses. Despite all this there survived in the new housing area a slaughter house and the old Co-op shop which for some unknown reason remained long after all the surrounding houses had gone.

I wonder if any of you worked for Collier's in King Edward Street where a lot of good things were made. Products of this local business can still be seen around the Town. When the building finally succumbed to the blight it was replaced by the 'famous' Stuart House which became the home of most of the council planners and executives. A very posh and expensive building which looked from the outside like a multi-storey car park and was certainly no improvement on the building it replaced. As the main council offices it lacked parking facilities for the public - perhaps they did not want the public to call. Things have not changed much with the new Town Hall extension!

Another area I have neglected to mention was that of Waterside. This area had houses, factories and pubs, and some of it still remains intact. The area never struck me as a very nice place to live but those who lived there probably thought differently. The area is now dominated by the concrete pillars which support the new Silk Road over the River Bollin.

Just a few final memories:

February 1950. A fire at Swindell's Mill in Vincent Street cost ten thousand pounds and it was so cold at the time the water froze in the fireman's hoses.

August 1961. The foundation stone was laid for the new church of St. John on Earlsway. In 1998 the church was demolished.

1960. Central Station was demolished. Lamaload Reservoir was built. The crematorium opened. In November Hibel Road Station and the Churnet Valley Railway line closed. Part of this line has recently been opened again at Cheddleton in Staffordshire by Cheddleton Railway Limited - a day visit there to travel once again in steam is a real must.

1962. The GPO tower was built on Sutton Common and one way traffic was introduced to the town. Richard Attenborough opened the new Boys' Club at Fermain.

1963. The big freeze when the temperature in January never rose above freezing point and the blizzards blocked all roads into the Town. A train was stranded at North Rode in the snow. Later in the year Mr Wadsworth gave the Boy Scouts their camping ground at Barnswood, Rushton. The building of Upton Priory Estate started.

You will all have your own memories of the Town. I hope that I have revived a few of them.

Colliers, King Edward Street.

Metalwork Class, 1953, with Mr Jardine, King's School.

CHAPTER TWELVE
THE PAST PRESENT AND FUTURE

Had I been permitted to choose just when I came into this world, I think I would not have chosen a different date. I have been fortunate to have lived in an age where I have not had to experience at first hand any wars. I have seen man's progress through the age of the motor car, the breaking of the sound barrier, the first space flight, a man on the moon, deisel and electric trains replacing steam and the career of the world's most famous footballer, Sir Stanley Matthews.

I experienced school days which gave me cigarette cards, marbles, and conkers when in season, whilst the opposite sex had skipping, hopscotch and top and whip; now replaced by the walkman, game boy computers and virtual pets. I went to school with dripping butties for my lunch, if I was lucky, not like today with a sanitised chocolate bar wrapped so well it is almost impossible to get it out of its wrapper. I even remember fondly the holes in my socks and my mother's regular use of the darning needle, not seen much today.

During my time on this earth I have made many friends through school and through work. I was in contact with over one thousand personnel whilst working at Parkside Hospital and many more through the Scout movement. I met with many more through my businesses, first teaching driving and then transporting over two thousand school children safely to and from school by coach. My service in the Royal Air Force and Civil Defence added to the numbers. Many friends of my own age will soon be collecting their pensions and free bus passes. I often wonder how they see the world today.

When I look back at my school days I think of the teachers and class mates, many of whom I have not seen since those days. The following are those who I recall were in the same class as myself at Kings in 1953. Miller, Oldem, Taylor, Hopley, Hurst, Hunter, Bateson, Bayley, Leigh, Gaskel, Munro, Parrott, Kendal, Davenport, Bowyer, McGrath, Brown, Mercer, Wood, Dearden, Burgess, Webb, Brook, Wild, Lawrence, Clark, Lopez, Brough, Unwin and Mills. My apologies to anyone I may have forgotten.

Whilst I was looking through some of my old photograph albums I came across photographs of the following friends. I wonder if you recognise yourself amongst them. The year would have been between 1950 and 1953: John Henshaw, Anetta Harte, Rodney Hawkyard, Marjorie White, Robin Dorey, Muriel Gould, John Armitage, Jaquline Scroggins, Keith Bradley, Ann Corbishley, Lamona Farish, Howard Collier, Pamela Hill, Kenneth Sykes, Christine Parrott, Margaret Harrison, Aileen Arden, Roslie Royston, Mary Bakewell, Marlene Selby, Dereck Oldham, Patricia Ann Wood, John Bowyer, Geoffrey Rose, John Bateson, Maureen Bateson, David Marsden, Jack Beck, Sheila Ripley, Valerie Simpson, Christine Cordell, Adna Jeffrey, John Bailey, Gordon Byrom, Philip Bailey, Marjorie Whittington, Judy Laidlaw, Patricia Wood, Margaret Nixon, Barry Trueman, and Jasper Hough.

In the 1970s I did an awful lot of travelling. I always found that the journey to and from a place was part of the interest unlike today when the main criteria seems to be to arrive by plane in the shortest possible time. You now arrive at your place in the sun and just laze around drinking British beer at British type bars, speaking English and eating fish and chips. The Brits seem to get drunk on the cheap wine and antagonise the locals with their outrageous behaviour and then fly back to 'Blighty'. They seem to lack any sense of adventure. The desire to explore seems to have faded in all but a few of our younger generation. It seems we have lost our way along with the loss of the British Empire.

I often sit and wonder just what is going wrong with this wonderful country of ours. We import timber from Scandinavia when we could grow all our own. Our farmers grow the best lamb in the world but we import lamb from New Zealand because it's cheaper. We close down all our coal mines and then import coal from Poland. We put a 70mph speed limit on our roads and then built cars capable of twice that speed.

It is even stranger that we design our cars with seat belts, air bags, crumple zones and side impact bars to make the driver feel safe to such an extent that they feel immune from injury. The result is that we kill and injure an increasing number of cyclists and pedestrians. I wonder if we will ever get our priorities right or are we resigned to the fact that five thousand fatalities a year on our roads is an acceptable figure for the freedom the car gives.

One of my greatest regrets was the need to demolish Ecolodge, the Country's first autonomous house which I designed and built in 1980. It was televised twice by the BBC and at the official opening of the house, our MP said it was forty years ahead of its time. It had solar panels, wind-powered electricity and gas from a methane digester fuelled by effluent, but it was not a saleable product due to the cheap cost of oil and coal. When it came to my moving house the land was worth more than the building! It later became Braeside Close, sporting six conventional bungalows. The one good thing was that the building was re-cycled and none of it finished up in a land fill site.

The present time has its good and its bad points but I look back at rooms with picture rails, high skirting boards, black leaded grates, and hallways decorated with stiff brown paper to combat sticky fingers. Will we ever see the return of the aspidistra in the hallway mounted on a tall wooden stand?

The new world has brought us TV, fast cars, space travel, mobile homes, cheap foreign travel and computers. It has also brought us global warming, acid rain, rising sea levels, holes in the ozone layer, extreme weather conditions, wars and malnutrition. And AIDs, BSE, and GM crops.

It has been said that Man's greatest invention was the wheel and no doubt that is true. The wheel was followed a long time later by the internal combustion engine, which lead to the scramble for control of the finite stocks of the world's oil and conflicts around the globe. This one invention may yet prove to be Man's most destructive invention, apart from the H bomb, and may eventually lead to our extinction.

Our headlong rush for so-called progess, perhaps now an unstoppable force, led as it is by big business, and driven by the desire for money, has given us a longer life expectancy, but at what cost. I strongly suspect that man is rushing into the destruction of his own planet and unless the next generation has a radical rethink and a change of direction I see no future for us. Our greed has already made many species extinct and it is entirely possible that Man will not be around to celebrate the start of the next millennium.

Meanwhile I shall continue in my retirement, enjoying my hobby creating woodland nature reserves for the 'lesser' species in the hope that the world will continue long after I have gone. I do hope the next generation will do a better job than my generation have done.

The End